Sarah C. [barcode] n.
May. 1946.

British Trees in Colour

First published in Great Britain by
Michael Joseph Ltd
52 Bedford Square, London wc 1
1973

ISBN 0 7181 1157 5

This book was designed and produced by
Rainbird Reference Books Limited
Marble Arch House, 44 Edgware Road
London w2, England

Designer: Ronald Clark

Printed by W. S. Cowell Ltd
Ipswich, Suffolk
Bound by Dorstel Press Ltd
Harlow, Essex

BRITISH TREES IN COLOUR

by Cyril Hart

Illustrations by Charles Raymond

Michael Joseph, London

Contents

Softwoods (plates 41–63)

Preface

Britain has a rich heritage of trees – some native, others introduced – some evergreen, others deciduous – in an exceptionally wide range of beauty, interest and utility. They enrich her gardens, parks, roadsides, hedgerows and watercourses; and many stand in arboreta, pinetums and forest gardens. Furthermore, untold numbers of trees clothe her national and private woodlands, wherein annual planting for commercial purposes is over one hundred million.

Conifers ('softwoods') are now extensively planted throughout Britain's woodlands – chiefly for economic reasons. This change from the traditional broad-leaved ('hardwood') trees is regretted by some people, but even constructive critics should concede that hardwoods, though they possess individual beauty, in mass during winter often present a sombre leafless picture, relieved only by the evergreen Holly, Yew, and climbing ivy.

Since the introduction of softwoods in mass much of Britain's sylvan scene has a patchwork cloak of many colours in all seasons. Her winters are relieved by the evergreen conifers and the hues of the bare larches, all of which supplement the Silver Birches and the carpets of decaying leaves. Early spring is heralded by the yellow lambs' tails of Hazel, the flower-haze of the elms, and the silver and yellow catkins of Sallow; while the buds and catkins of the Alders continue to display a purple sheen. Later appear the changing greens of the larches and birch. April and May bring the flower-haze of Ash, the fruit-haze of elms, and the bud-haze of Beech and oak, all followed by the first flushes and deepening foliage of these and most other broad-leaved trees, supplemented by the white blossoms of Wild Cherry and Blackthorn.

Throughout summer, Britain's trees are crowned with a mantle of needles and leaves of many shades of green, sometimes contrasted by faintly blue or silver sheens. Here and there the scene is enriched with the blossoms of Hawthorn, Rowan, Whitebeam, Crab Apple and Guelder Rose. When during this season the hardwoods are in such mass that, particularly from afar, their greens are difficult to distinguish, the secondary flush of foliage (for example, of some oaks) gives a little contrast and relief to the scene. Thereafter, interest and colour are added by resplendent berries, and by fruits which vary from the pink seed-pods of Spindle Tree to clusters of red-tinged wings of Sycamore. Before summer is forgotten, and as some compensation for the shortening days, the glory of autumn falls on the deciduous trees – a rich mingling of browns, russet-reds and golden-yellows – heralding the fall of fruits, cones, seeds and spent foliage. Ceaselessly the rhythm of the beauty of woods and trees recurs as the seasons wax and wane; and, as Emerson noted, 'a perennial festival is dressed'.

Year by year, many of the vast coniferous forests planted in the last five decades pass from unprepossessing youth and adolescence to handsome maturity. Though some people who remember our old woodlands, predominantly broad-leaved, are sad at their partial passing, on the generation that knows only the newer trees as they mature, the magic of the sylvan scene casts its spell as powerfully as on their forebears.

Thus our trees, both broad-leaved and coniferous, are a delight to many, and the objectives of this book are to assist the reader to identify and to appreciate a wide and representative range of them. The work arose through my suggestion to the producers that a treatise on British trees in colour might be an acceptable companion to their renowned book, *The Concise British Flora in Colour* (1965) by the Reverend W. Keble Martin. The illustrations herein are the work of Charles Raymond. It is to be hoped that the reader will endorse my warm appreciation and admiration of the excellency of his painstaking and beautiful artistry. His co-operation has been of the highest order, and to both of us the task of preparing this book has been one of pleasure.

My choice of forty broad-leaved trees and twenty-three conifers has been based upon experience in teaching silviculture in the Estate Management Department of the Royal Agricultural College at Cirencester, and in particular upon my observations here in the Royal Forest of Dean. The selection has also been made to interest the arboriculturist with his specimens or groups in parks and gardens, and the silviculturist tending his traditional woods or more recent plantations. Purposefully represented among the conifers are three two-needled pines, and one each of those pines having three and five needles. Dawn Redwood ('fossil tree') and Leyland Cypress are included because interest in them is increasing. In the text, I have attempted to provide the chief means of identification, the main features, and other points of interest. But I have rarely touched upon folk-lore or legend relative to our trees, and not at all upon their usage as boundary markers in ancient land charters and their rôle in the origin of many of our place-names. Interesting information of this kind is readily available in: Miles Hadfield, *British Trees: A Guide for Everyman* (Dent, 1957); *Landscape with Trees* (Country Life Ltd, 1967); and H. L. Edlin, *Wayside and Woodland Trees* (Warne, 1971).

The producers are warmly thanked for their encouragement throughout the preparation of the book and for their care with its layout and production. Appreciation is also acknowledged to the following who have kindly assisted on some technical points in the text: Miles Hadfield, Herbert Edlin and Alan Mitchell. The Forestry Commission have also been most helpful. Finally, I wish to place on record my thanks for pleasure and inspiration derived from studying the beautiful water colours of trees of the late John Patten which he presented to the Royal Agricultural College.

Cyril Hart
Chenies,
Coleford,
Forest of Dean,
Gloucestershire GL16 8DT
15 April 1973

Introduction

The trees herein are grouped into two sections which correspond with the two natural divisions of all trees found in Britain. The first, the angiosperms, are represented here by the dicotyledons; the form of their leaves gives the class one name, broad-leaved trees, the structure of their wood another, hardwoods – though a few are soft-wooded (Lime, willow). The second division is that of gymnosperms, comprised of the class broadly termed conifers; the structure of their wood gives rise to their general classification as softwoods – though Yew has a very hard wood. Within the above two subdivisions come the families signified by the termination -aceae; for example, Fagaceae, the Beech family, which includes six genera, among them the oak genus, *Quercus*, and Sweet Chestnut, *Castanea*.

The final unit of classification is the species, one or more of which form the genus; thus we have *Quercus robur*, English Oak, and the other species of *Quercus*. The specific names have varying meanings; for example, *alba*, white, *glutinosus*, covered with a sticky exudation, and *grandis*, large. Occasionally we have variations that are sufficiently distinct from the typical form of the species to warrant separate description; for example, *Populus nigra* 'Italica', Lombardy Poplar. Hybrids, the offspring of two distinct parents, have arisen by chance in Britain, namely, Hybrid Larch and Leyland Cypress. Many hybrid poplars have been produced by design and now play a moderate rôle in British forestry. Each tree herein is described botanically by the name of the genus, followed by the species, and where relevant the varietal name. A suffix, usually abbreviated – for example, L. (for Linnaeus), refers to the botanist (Carl Linnaeus of Sweden, 1707–1778) who first published the name used. Alternative acceptable names or synonyms of the trees are also provided.

Only two of Britain's conifers (other than the scrubby Juniper) are indigenous – Scots Pine and Yew. Most of her more common broad-leaved trees are native. Some other trees have been in Britain so long that understandably people consider them to be native – for example, European Larch, Norway Spruce, Sycamore, Sweet Chestnut and plane.

There are many exotic conifers which have found an important place in British forestry. As well as European Larch and Norway Spruce from Europe, established from the north-west coast of America are Douglas Fir, Western Hemlock, Western Red Cedar, Sitka Spruce, Redwood, Wellingtonia and Lodgepole Pine. From other parts of the globe have come Japanese Larch and Corsican Pine. A quite recent introduction (1948) from China has been Dawn Redwood ('fossil tree').

Identification of Trees
Broad-leaved trees (hardwoods) are mostly deciduous, i.e. they shed their

leaves in winter; exceptions herein are Evergreen Oak and Holly. Conifers (softwoods) are chiefly evergreen; exceptions herein are the larches and Dawn Redwood. It should be noted that the foliage of a tree termed 'evergreen' may in fact be some other colour than green, e.g. golden or blue; also, the needles or leaves of evergreens remain alive for only two, three or more years, and then fade to brown or yellow before they unobtrusively fall.

In identifying a tree one looks to its general form, the bark, twigs, buds, leaf scars, leaves or needles, flowers and fruit. Trees vary widely in botanical characteristics, colour, tone and texture; and they change some of these characteristics throughout the seasons in their progress through the production of bud to foliage, and fruit. Aids to identification likewise differ throughout the year – in some species only the bark and the form are constant.

Thus in winter, a typical deciduous broad-leaved tree has bare branches, with only form, bark, twig, bud and perhaps persistent fruits to reveal its identity. In spring, the same tree will display bursting leaf-buds, but the first flush of leaves may be smaller than or of a colour different from those typical of later months. In summer, identification is comparatively easy, because the foliage is usually supplemented by flowers and fruits. Through autumn the leaves, though changing in colour, and the maturing fruits or their remnants in varying forms, aid identification. The time of leafing, flowering and fruiting varies according to species, location and climate.

Conifers are comparatively easy to identify, particularly the evergreens with their almost constant foliage. Seasonal changes occur through the production of shoots and flowers, and the developing and maturing cones. The few deciduous conifers herein (the larches and Dawn Redwood) are bereft of foliage in winter, yet other characteristics readily reveal their identity.

The important characteristics to aid identification are given below. There, and in the main text, description of colour is usually an approximation – shoot and bud, sometimes bark, are generally much more brightly pigmented on the surfaces that are exposed to the sun; and the greens of the foliage are so varied as to sometimes defy exact description.

WINTER TWIGS AND BUDS: Winter twigs of broad-leaved trees are of varying form – from round to angular – from straight to zigzag – and they may be hairy or otherwise, slender (birch), stout and grey (Ash), pith chambered (Elder), or pith laminated (Walnut). Some trees, for example poplars, Rowan, and larches, produce 'short shoots' or 'spurs', which develop only a small fraction of an inch each year. As compared with the long shoots they are thick and wrinkled, and later generally bear a tuft of leaves or flowers at the end. The arrangement of the winter (or resting) growth buds may be opposite (Ash), alternate (Beech), or spiral (oak); they may be round (Lime), squat (Hazel), conical (Beech), appressed (Hornbeam, willow), hairy (Hazel), or large and sticky (Horse Chestnut). They have a wide range of colour, for example – green (Hazel, Sycamore), brown (Beech, Horse Chestnut), purple (Alder), red (maple, Lime), and black (Ash). The number and arrangement of the bud scales are pertinent. So too are the shape and markings of the scar left by the fallen leaf-stalk, which has many different forms – for example, large and conspicuous in Horse Chestnut and Walnut, and small and narrow in birch. The flower buds, as distinct from the leaf-buds, are not always easy to differentiate until development proceeds. Important in conifers is the bud-shape, and whether or not the buds are resin-coated.

LEAVES: In hardwoods the arrangement of the leaves follows that of the bud, and the leaves vary in shape whether in simple or compound form. Simple leaves may be linear or lanceolate (some willows), oval (Beech), cordate (Lime), obcordate (Alder), triangular (birch, most poplars), or asymmetric (elm). Compound leaves may be digitate (Horse Chestnut) or pinnate (Ash, Rowan, Elder, Walnut). Palmately lobed leaves include those of maple, Sycamore and plane. The length, width, venation and number of leaflets are diverse; so too are the margins, which may be entire, wavy, toothed (serrated), or lobed (oak). If the leaf is stalkless it is termed sessile. The surface of the leaf may be smooth (without hairs, i.e. glabrous) or hairy (pubescent, as in Elm), and in colour may vary between the upper and under surface (Whitebeam). The colours of most leaves change between flushing and falling; for example, some poplars, Walnut and oak open as a light khaki or brown colour and develop through varying shades of green to their autumn hues. Beech leaves, which on opening lay a carpet of light red bud-coverings, are light translucent green in spring while in autumn they are golden or russet. The leaves of Hornbeam turn a rich yellow, while those of Whitebeam, green above and grey-white underneath, fall in autumn to provide a wrinkled carpet of purple-grey hue.

Two more points should be noted about leaves. Those low down on a broad-leaved tree (particularly leaves on suckers) are often larger than the typical ones above. And leaves in the seedling stage differ, on most trees, from those typical of the species; each kind of tree has its particular germination pattern. Oak, for example, always has its two cotyledons (seed-leaves) in the soil, but Beech expands its two broad green seed-leaves above ground. The cotyledons are followed by the primary ('juvenile') foliage which in general is different from the secondary or 'adult' kind usually developed in the second year of growth. Thus, a seedling Ash has three or four kinds of leaf: first the long oval seed-leaf, then an individual juvenile leaf, next a compound leaf with only three leaflets, and finally the adult form of compound-pinnate leaf, having many leaflets. When most conifers are in the seedling stage they have a number of seed-needles in the form of a little whorl or rosette; solitary needles always follow and often the typical needle formation does not develop until the second year. 'Juvenile' foliage is found on all terminal shoots in larches, Dawn Redwood and true cedars.

In conifers, from the foliage point of view the main aid to identification is the needles (more correctly termed leaves). In pines they appear grouped in basal sheaths, when their number and length and colour are important. Some conifers have short needles in rosettes or in horizontal ranks. Others have scale-like leaves either in fern-like sprays or in cord-like growths. By their 'adult' needles, the conifers herein can be divided for the purpose of identification into four simple categories:

I	With long needles in bundles. *Pinus* (all evergreen)		
	In twos	In threes	In fives
	Scots Pine Corsican Pine Lodgepole Pine	Monterey Pine	Weymouth Pine
II	With numerous short needles in rosettes		
	Deciduous	Evergreen	
	The larches	Atlas Cedar Deodar Cedar Lebanon Cedar	
III	With short needles spirally arranged, sometimes seemingly in horizontal ranks		
	Deciduous	Evergreen	
	Dawn Redwood	Spruces Grand Fir Douglas Fir Western Hemlock Redwood Yew Noble Fir (needles are massed on top of twig)	
IV	With scale-like leaves (all evergreen)		
	In fern-like sprays	In cord-like growths	
	Lawson Cypress Western Red Cedar Leyland Cypress	Wellingtonia	

Some aid to identification of conifers is obtained from the smell of crushed foliage, to which references are made in the text. Needle colour is also important, but is not constant in ornamental varieties.

FLOWERS: A fascinating botanical characteristic of trees is their flowers. In broad-leaves, male (♂) and female (♀) flowers are in some species borne on separate trees (*dioecious*, e.g. willow, poplar), and in other species on the same tree (*monoecious*, and sometimes *hermaphrodite*, i.e. both sexes in one flower, e.g. Rowan, Elm). In conifers, both sexes are borne separately, though usually on the same tree (Yew is an exception). The variety of flowers is great: they range in the broad-leaves from the inconspicuous green and yellow 'catkins' of oak and the tiny red female flowers of Hazel, to the purple-tinted tufts of Ash or dark purplish-red tufts of elms, and to the large spiked inflorescence of Horse Chestnut. Some broad-leaves flower before the leaves appear, for example, Elm, Sallow, Hazel, Alder, Hornbeam, Blackthorn, Ash and Norway Maple. The flowers of conifers are usually female conelets and male pollen-bearing catkins which are simply short-lived clusters of stamens. They are generally small and set somewhat inconspicuously amid the foliage; thus they often escape notice. Some are very attractive – for example, in European Larch the male flowers are small bright clusters of anthers bearing showers of golden pollen, while the female 'larch roses' are rich pink in colour and have the form – in miniature – of the later cone; in Noble Fir the clusters of deep purple male catkins are a delight to behold. The age at which trees begin to produce flowers and fruits is very variable. The shedding of pollen generally takes place in spring or summer; in the true cedars it is liberated in autumn.

FRUITS AND SEEDS: The arrangement of the female flowers, whether in broad-leaves or conifers, obviously decides the arrangement of the subsequent fruit or cone and seeds. For example, female flowers of Elm and Ash being in clusters, it follows that the fruits (respectively, soft transparent roundish wings, and hard elongated 'keys') are found likewise. Fruits of broad-leaves are in wide variety – from the small nuts of Beech and Hazel to large chestnuts, and from the small berries of Hawthorn, Blackthorn, Spindle and Dogwood to the double-samaras of maples and Sycamore. There are also the woody 'cone' and winged seeds of Alder, the acorn, the cherry, the 'bobble' of plane, the hair-tufted seeds of poplar and willow, and the fruits with bracts – Lime and Hornbeam.

In conifers the fruit is nearly always a hard woody cone, bearing one- or two-winged seeds at the base of each scale; in contrast, Yew has a fleshy fruit – a seed surrounded by an aril. The cones vary from the small round structure of Lawson Cypress and the small 'Grecian urn' of Western Red Cedar, to the pendulous large and scaly cone of Weymouth

Pine and the erect 'barrels' of true cedars and silver firs. Among many
other kinds, there are the 'whiskered' cone of Douglas Fir and the
crinkled-scale cone of Sitka Spruce. Most cones take one year to ripen;
almost all pines take two years. Some disintegrate on the tree leaving
only a central spike (true cedars and some firs); other cones fall entire
(spruces and pines), but often their seeds have been dispersed.

The seeds of conifers show an interesting range of form and size, an idea
of which can be obtained by comparison with the numbers that go to
make up one pound by weight – from almost one thousand to more than
one hundred thousand. Often a handful of seed may represent many acres
of potential forest.

BARK: In youth, trees usually have a thin, smooth and green bark which
only later changes to a typical form and colour. Thus a single tree may
show at different stages of its growth, quite distinct and even contrasting
patterns, colours and thicknesses. A few trees (for example, Beech) continue to have a thin and smooth bark, but others when older may develop
bark of sometimes greater thicknesses which is scaly (Sitka Spruce),
patchy (plane), or horizontally ribboned (birch, cherry). Other trees of
greater age develop bark which is furrowed (Douglas Fir) or ridged and
patterned – for example oak (cubed), Walnut (diamond-shaped) and
Sweet Chestnut (spiral). Corky bark may be found on young Elm and
Field Maple, while the bark of Redwood and Wellingtonia is very thick,
spongy and fibrous. The colour of some bark changes as the age increases,
and may differ according to the direction of exposure – oak, Beech,
Sycamore and larch have sometimes in part a pink or purplish sheen. The
bark of Beech and Hornbeam has a distinct metallic appearance, while
they (and the bark of other trees) may be coloured or discoloured by
varying shades of lichen. Resin blisters usually develop in Douglas Fir,
Grand Fir and Noble Fir.

FORM AND OUTLINE: Many trees can from a distance be identified at sight
by their form, outline or the disposition of their branches, coupled with
their general colour. Much will depend on whether the tree is growing
healthily in open conditions, or in a woodland, or in a wind-swept place.
An isolated oak is likely to have a broad-spreading crown and a short,
thick bole, whereas one of the same age growing in a wood will have a
much narrower crown and (the silviculturist would expect) a taller and
branchless trunk. A young Scots Pine, wherever grown, will have a
roughly conical outline and may be clothed with foliage from ground
level; whereas an old tree will usually bear a rugged crown springing
from the top of a branchless orange-coloured trunk.

Broad-leaved trees generally have a less formal growth than conifers
and a more oval crown of branches, and are thus more static in shape and

outline. Conifers tend to have a pointed shape and a more formal habit of growth. The characteristic of the top shoot (leader) of a conifer is often helpful, particularly in Lawson Cypress (drooping), Western Red Cedar (erect) and Western Hemlock (whip-like, pendent). Pines, Grand Fir and spruces have their branches in distinct whorls. The form of a tree must be interpreted with regard to all these characteristics.

WOOD (TIMBER): The character of wood is peculiar to each kind of tree. It is an intricate study which lies beyond the scope of this book, but in the text a brief description is given of each timber's superficial appearance, and its uses.

Trees are an essential ingredient of Britain's natural beauty, forming her delightful sylvan landscape. Identification and study of them will be rewarding, and will make possible enlightened comment as to their care and replenishment. People depend on trees: they *expect* them to be there. But in a modern industrial country trees are dependent on people. They cannot be taken for granted: they live long but are not immortal. Unless there is new planting, generations to come will not enjoy the treasure-house of trees passed down by the people of the 18th and 19th centuries. Only care and foresight will perpetuate Britain's sylvan heritage.

Glossary

appressed	lying flat against
aril	fleshy seed coat or covering such as on the fruit of the yew
auricle	a small ear-like formation at a leaf base
bract	a leaf-like structure arising at the base of a flower or of part of an inflorescence
coppice	the crop of shoots which grow after some trees are cut down
cordate	heart-shaped
corymb	a flattish topped flower cluster, the outer flowers usually opening first
cyme	a broad flattened flower cluster, the central flowers opening first
digitate	a leaf divided into five or more leaflets, hand-like
dioecious	bearing the male and female flowers on separate trees
epicormic (shoots)	arising from the outer layers of wood
flush	bud burst
flute	furrow down the trunk
glabrous	hairless
glaucous	bluish colour; covered with bloom
heartwood	the central aged part of the wood which no longer carries sap
inflorescence	the arrangement of the flowers but often used to denote the flower cluster
leader	the main shoot on the principal stem
lenticel	breathing cell in the bark
linear	slender
monoecious	bearing the male and female flowers separately but on the same tree
node	the leaf joint with the stem

ob-	obversely or oppositely
ovate	egg-shaped in outline (two dimensional)
ovoid	egg-shaped (three dimensional)
palmate	lobed or divided from a central point into a hand-like formation
panicle	an indeterminate branched flower cluster with stalked flowers
pinnate	opposite leaflets along a common stalk
pubescent	a covering of fine short hairs
samara	a one-sided, winged fruit
sapwood	the outer younger part of the wood in which the sap flows
sessile	without a stalk
stipule	a leaf-like growth at the base of the leaf-stalk
stomata	breathing pores
strobile	(cone) flower of a conifer
suberose	corky
umbo	the central boss of a cone scale

Index

Numbers refer to plate numbers

The Plates

1

Acer campestre L. **Field Maple** ACERACEAE

Deciduous Native

The Field Maple is a small tree that may attain a height of 20 to 70 feet, but is most familiar as a mere bush of the wayside or hedgerow, particularly on chalk or lime-stone formations. When displaying its colourful winged fruits, it is a very pretty tree.

The slender twigs are light brown, and after the first year may have a layer of cork that projects outwards in conspicuous irregular vertical ridges. The opposite winter buds are brown, with short hairs on the scales. The leaves as they unfold are often tinged with a rosy or pinky red, and have a leaf-stalk which is usually tinged with red or brown. They are small (rarely more than 2 inches in length or breadth) and have normally five rounded lobes. They are dull green above but paler green below, and turn to a bright golden shade in autumn.

The erect, few-flowered inflorescence comprises small pale greenish-yellow flower usually of both sexes, which open in May. Their two-lobed ovary develops into a double 'samara' – an almost straight pair of broad-winged 'keys' about $\frac{1}{2}$–1 inch long, with their bases joined together. In summer these 'keys' are often tinged with crimson, afterwards turning brown as they ripen.

The bark is light brown, sometimes with a dull orange tinge, smooth at first but becoming darker and furrowed with small scales which flake off. The wood is pale brown, hard, tough and strong. When sufficiently large, it is ideal for carving or for turning into bowls and platters.

2

Acer platanoides L. **Norway Maple** ACERACEAE

Deciduous

Norway Maple was introduced from Scandinavia in the seventeenth century, and has since enriched Britain's scenery with its bright spring blossom and rich autumn foliage. In height it reaches some 75 feet.

The twigs are stout and shiny, generally tinged with red before turning brown. The small winter buds are set oppositely, and are bluntly pointed, with shiny reddish-tinged scales. The leaves when unfolding show rust-red tints. They are palmately five-lobed, sharply angled, bright green, rather shiny, with a long slender stalk which is tinged with red and contains milky sap. In autumn the leaves show a standard good yellow, and later brilliant orange-brown colours for a brief spell.

The greenish-yellow flowers of both sexes are found together in an erect or spreading inflorescence in the form of a corymbose panicle, and appear in early April before the leaves unfold. The fruit consists of two winged seeds – the well-known double 'samara' (or 'keys'), set at an angle of about 160°. They are green at first, becoming brown before they spin away.

The bark is thin, dark grey to brown, with short, smooth, narrow, and shallow fissures. The wood is white or greyish, fine-textured, hard and fairly heavy. It is used for furniture and turnery goods. If cut when dormant in winter and early spring the tree freely 'bleeds' its sugary sap.

Foresters sometimes cultivate Norway Maple for timber, but more often their chief objective is to form with it an attractive belt around other tree-crops. Unfortunately it suffers much harm, particularly in the crown, from the grey squirrel, which is attracted by its sweet sap.

3

Acer pseudoplatanus L. **Sycamore** ACERACEAE

Deciduous

Sycamore, an attractive tall tree with masses of mat green foliage and pleasant summer fruits, was brought from France during the Middle Ages. It seeds profusely and thrives in Britain like a native tree.

The young green, paired twigs turn light brown during the first year. The opposite winter buds are green and have a leaf-scar below. The leaves often have a red or orange tint on opening, and have five broad, coarsely-toothed lobes, and are up to 8 inches broad, blunt-pointed, with long reddish stalks which contain watery sap. They are deep green on the upper surface and pale bluish-green underneath – which underside is conspicuous when the foliage billows in the wind. Often the leaves are disfigured by 'tar spots' (caused by the fungus *Rhytisma acerinum*). In autumn the leaves turn a drab colour, but occasionally yellow.

The bi-sexual greenish-yellow flowers, which open late in May, are in pendent panicles of fifty or more, with the youngest towards the tip. The fruits hang in bunches comprised of the well-known winged double 'samara' (or 'keys') set at an angle of about 90°, and green at first, then handsomely tinged with crimson, becoming brown before the air currents spin them far afield.

On young trees the bark is very pale grey and smooth but later breaks into irregular fawn-brown scales which flake off. In some districts of Britain the trunks have in part a purplish sheen. The odourless wood is of a clean appearance, creamy to yellowish-white, moderately heavy and fairly hard. Its uses include furniture, textile rollers and turned kitchen utensils such as bowls, spoons and platters. If the wood has a rippled grain, it commands a very high price for veneers. When cut in January to early spring, the tree profusely 'bleeds' its watery sap.

Silviculturists find Sycamore an excellent shelterbelt tree. It grows freely from self-sown seed and is an important timber tree, though much spoiled by grey squirrels, which peel the bark in order to obtain the sweet sap.

4

Aesculus hippocastanum L. **Horse Chestnut** HIPPOCASTANACEAE

Deciduous

Horse Chestnut, a native of the Balkans and Asia Minor, was brought to Britain in the sixteenth century, and is found usually as a magnificent spreading park and avenue tree, though it also appears self-sown in some woodlands. The display of prominent showy white blossoms on its arching branches is its chief attribute.

The shoots are stout, becoming pale grey or brown, with large horse-shoe-shaped scars left by the fallen leaf-stalks. The brown winter buds are large, sharply pointed and thickly coated with resin. The shoots flush in March and the foliage soon puts on the appearance of a damaged wing of a bird, later expanding magnificently. The leaves consist of from five to seven leaflets with serrated margins, and palmately arranged from a long stalk. Each leaflet becomes broader towards the tip, then suddenly narrows to a point; the largest may reach almost a foot in length. The upper surface is a dismal dark green and hairless, the lower is covered with woolly down which soon disperses. In autumn the leaves change to yellow and gold, or in parts to red.

The handsome candelabra-like inflorescence, with hermaphrodite flowers, is erect in mid-May, and may exceed a foot in height, having more than a hundred white flowers that have delicate petal edges frilled in variable patterns and a yellow blotch that turns pale crimson. The inedible fruit, one or more lustrous red-brown seeds ('conkers'), ripens in early autumn within a tough, thick, leathery and spiky husk which has changed from pale green to dark brown.

The bark is dark greyish-brown, smooth in young trees but later breaking into unevenly sized and shaped pink-brown scales which are eventually shed. The white wood is too soft and brittle to have much practical use.

The trunk is often fluted and spreading somewhat at the base. Though self-sown trees are common, it is an ornamental rather than a woodland tree.

5

Alnus incana (L.) Moench., **Grey Alder** BETULACEAE

Deciduous

The Grey Alder, introduced from Central Europe in 1780, is distinguished from the native Alder, *A. glutinosa* (L.) Gaertn., by its grey bark, downy (not glutinous) young shoots, and pointed leaves, grey beneath, and its tendency to sucker vigorously. It thrives on even fairly dry areas and has been chosen for illustration because it is less common.

The native Alder is a moderately-sized tree with a narrow crown and short, spreading branches and grows in moist places, usually alongside streams, rivers, ponds and lakes.

Its winter buds, borne alternately on reddish-brown twigs which are rather tacky in their green state, are distinctly stalked and have a purple waxy bloom. The alternate leaves (about 2–3 inches broad and long) are either round or slightly obcordate; they are dark green, have a toothed margin, and are slightly tacky as they unfold, hence the specific name, *glutinosa*, sticky. Both sexes of flowers are borne on the same tree, before the leaves open. The male catkins are oblong, drooping, purplish or reddish-brown becoming yellow, and about an inch long. The female catkins are small, cylindrical and purplish-brown; after pollination they enlarge to a green oval or spherical shape, later becoming a brown woody cone-like structure about half an inch long, which opens during the winter permitting the numerous small winged seeds to escape. Many of the empty 'cones' persist on the tree well into spring. At first the bark is fairly smooth and greenish-brown, but later becomes fissured and dark grey. A height of over 75 feet can be attained; the tree is usually harvested before this, whereupon coppice shoots arise from the stool.

Alder is rarely planted – it springs up mainly from seeds that have been carried by water. It will grow in conditions of wetness of soil which few trees will tolerate. The timber is reddish, but bright orange when first cut, mellowing to dull brown. The wood is strong and easily worked but not naturally durable. Its uses include paper pulp and turnery goods such as broom heads and cheap tool handles. In earlier days it was valued for soles of clogs and for charcoal used in the manufacture of gun-powder.

An interesting point about Alder is that it bears on its roots curious nodules, like those of leguminous plants, in which live a bacterium, enabling it to take soluble nitrogen salts out of the inert nitrogen of the air; consequently the soils on which Alder grows are remarkably fertile. The tree is sometimes planted as a fire-break in plantations.

6

Betula pendula Roth. **Silver** or **Warty Birch** BETULACEAE

Deciduous Native

Silver Birch, or Warty Birch, seeds itself so freely in some areas that it is often ignored. However, it is a graceful, slender tree, usually with attractive white bark; and its timber is quite useful. It is less common than Hairy Birch in the north-west of Britain.

Its purplish-brown twigs are slender, whippy and harsh to the touch, and often pendulous. The young shoots are glabrous and bear little pale-coloured rough warts. The small brown winter buds are alternate, many-scaled and pointed. In early spring they expand to show in mass a purplish bloom before the leaflets, first light-green, then emerald, unfold. The leaves are about one inch broad and somewhat triangular, with a double-toothed margin, always sharply pointed, and hairless but often rough to the touch. They usually turn yellow before falling.

The yellow male catkins droop like lambs' tails, whereas the smaller pale-green female catkins are club-shaped and stand erect until they enlarge and become semi-mature, when they hang down. They open just after the leaves, and by August or September myriads of small winged seeds are produced and released on the winds.

The tough, waxy bark is purplish-brown in young trees, with horizontal bands of lenticels, but on older trees the smooth, papery, peeling bark of the upper part is silver-white, with black diamond-shaped markings, and the base becomes increasingly rough and blackened. On many a tree, growths termed witches' brooms will be found. The wood is tough, hard, clean and smooth, very pale brown or cream in colour, with a dull surface. Its uses include turnery goods such as brush backs, reels and toys, and paper pulp. The branches are used for besom-heads and horse jumps.

The Hairy Birch, *B. pubescens* Ehrh., with short and soft downy twigs and grey or cherry-like bark, is the second of Britain's two tall species of native birch. Hybridization and introgression occur between the two species. The terms 'white birch' and 'silver birch', and the obsolete scientific name *Betula alba*, have been applied to both of them. Few silviculturists make any distinctions between the birches.

Planting birch for timber has seldom been worthwhile economically: the millions growing in Britain's woods are nearly all self-sown. Foresters value the tree for its useful light cover, providing dappled shade which usually enables better trees, interplanted among the birches, to respond. It is a useful natural pioneer tree, adapted to colonize open land, and it coppices freely. In plantations.care must be taken to remove whippy birch trees that thrash and damage more desirable species.

7

Carpinus betulus L. **Hornbeam** CORYLACEAE

Deciduous Native

Hornbeam in winter is frequently passed by as beech, to which it has many resemblances except that the trunk is nearly always fluted and the buds on the young shoots are slightly appressed. At other seasons the curious fruiting catkins and the saw-toothed margins of the leaves which follow them, help in differentiation. Hornbeam is most frequently seen in the south-eastern and eastern counties of Britain, usually as a one-time coppiced or pollarded (often gnarled) medium-sized tree, but isolated specimens can sometimes be found in the most unexpected places.

The young shoots are very slender and turn from green to brown. They carry pale brown slender winter buds, set alternately, and slightly bent inwards on the younger shoots. The 1–2 inch long leaves, usually ovate and with more prominent parallel veins than beech, have sharply and doubly saw-toothed margins, and are dull green on top, paler and yellower underneath. They turn a rich yellow in autumn, and on young trees below a height of about 10 feet the spent brown leaves often persist throughout the winter.

The flowers appear in April along with the opening leaves. The pendent green male catkins, borne on the previous year's twigs, carry about ten stamens, on filaments divided below the anthers, which are orange in colour when they ripen. The female catkins, borne with the current season's growth, are much shorter than the males, and have slender crimson styles protruding from beneath long, narrow, recurving bracts, each of which carries two flowers. The small nut-like fruits, hard, flattened, and ribbed, are subtended by a large three-lobed or dagger-shaped papery appendage consisting of bract and bracteoles (secondary bracts) fused together. They ripen by October and persist after the leaves fall, draping the tree in brown.

The bole and some branches are usually fluted or prominently ribbed and have smooth, pale grey bark, often with a bright metallic sheen. The almost white wood is very hard, heavy and tough – hence its name which means 'horny tree'. It was formerly used for ox-yokes, cogs, mallets and wooden screws, and still serves as butchers' chopping blocks.

Hornbeam makes a good hedge. It is becoming less plentiful in woods because many of its habitats are being taken to raise crops of more profitable forest trees.

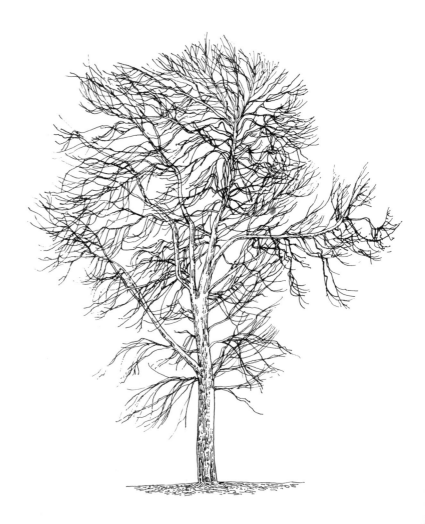

8

Castanea sativa Mill. **Sweet Chestnut** FAGACEAE

Deciduous

Sweet Chestnut (or Spanish Chestnut) native to the Mediterranean region, was introduced to Britain by the Romans as a source of nuts for food. It was abundant in the Forest of Dean by the eleventh century. As a stately tree it reaches some 100 feet in height.

The twigs are smooth or slightly downy, angular (five-sided), bear prominent lenticels, and are shiny olive-green to purplish-brown. The roundish winter buds are set alternately on little edges, and yellowish-green to brown. The leaves are bronze to khaki when opening, and long (often up to 9 inches), with sharply toothed margins, and veins which continue as bristles beyond the teeth.

Both male and female flowers lie on a slender yellow spike (that resembles a pipe-cleaner), the females being at its base; they open in July. The edible fruit ('chestnut') ripens during October in a green husk (cupule) which is clad in a mass of green sharp spikes. The brown nuts are usually in threes, and sometimes infertile.

In young trees the bark is smooth and greyish-green, but with age it becomes greyish-brown and deeply fissured, the fissures at the base of the trunk often forming either a left-hand or a right-hand spiral up to several feet. Some trees carry burrs which are found high up the bole. The wood has the strength and durability of oak, with a thinner sapwood; but whereas oak has conspicuous radiating (medullary) rays, those of chestnut are very fine and virtually invisible. It is apt to be 'shaky' (having radial or circular cracks), or to have spiral grain, but it has the important property of being easily split (cleft). It finds a ready sale for chestnut fencing, hop poles, posts and stakes. When large the wood is often a substitute for oak in furniture and in buildings.

Chestnut is frequently grown as a coppice crop. It thrives on warm, sandy soils, but is unhappy on most calcareous formations.

9

Cornus sanguinea L. **Dogwood** CORNACEAE

Deciduous Native

Dogwood is usually no more than a bush, but it can form a small tree. It is at home on the very dry chalk escarpment, but likely to be found infrequently on most lime-rich soils, either in isolation or as part of a hedgerow, thicket or game covert.

Its slender blood-red twigs carry the even more slender winter buds. The lower bark is greenish-grey. The opposite leaves are oval, 1–2 inches long, with prominent curved veins. They are among the first trees to show leaf – pale green in early March. In autumn they assume the same deep red shade as the twigs.

The small bi-sexual white flowers, which open in June, are in clusters (a corymb), and have an unpleasant odour. The fruit, a small berry, green at first, and later glossy black, lies in clusters. The fleshy parts of the berries are exceedingly bitter and each holds a hard seed.

Dogwood suckers freely and can build up dense thickets. Its white wood, though rarely large, is tough and smooth, and was traditionally used as skewers: the odd name arises from 'dog' – a sharp spike.

10

Corylus avellana L. **Hazel** CORYLACEAE

Deciduous Native

Hazel is rarely allowed to develop into a tree. Usually it thrives as a small shrub or bush, forming undergrowth or low coppice in woodlands, or as an unwanted component of a tended hedgerow.

The straight downy grey-brown twigs carry small winter buds set alternately, which are brown at first and green by February. The leaves are alternate, broad and roundish, with doubly toothed margins, and end in a little short tip. In autumn they change to brown, and finally pale yellow.

The yellow, pliant male catkins, drooping like lambs' tails, appear from January, having developed through winter from being little grey-green 'cylinders'. The female flower is much less conspicuous, being a small bud-like structure from which obtrude several fine crimson stigmas. The fruit is the well known hazel-nut, with a white 'kernel' enclosed in a shell that stands in a leafy cup often longer than the nut, and which together change from green to dark brown by autumn.

The bark is smooth and shining, and a brownish-red to greenish-brown, with conspicuous horizontal lenticels. On stouter stems the bark becomes silver-grey with a soft brownish tint. The wood is mid-brown in colour, strong and hard. Most uses of hazel have been in its round or cleft state, in old crafts that have lately almost died out – particularly that of wattle-hurdle making, and for wattle in house-building. It is still the traditional species for pea-sticks, bean-rods, hoops, heathering for hedge-laying, withes (for tying), and for some crates. Once a valuable element in rural economy, Hazel today is usually removed by foresters so that more profitable forest crops can be grown. Many people regret the gradual passing of a lovely form of woodland, which incidentally often harbours prim-roses, wild anemones, violets, bluebells and campion. They also regret the loss of the ancient traditional crafts of the underwood worker – as interesting as those of the charcoal-burner and the chair-bodger.

11

Crataegus monogyna Jacq. **Hawthorn, May** ROSACEAE

Deciduous Native

Hawthorn, a small tree, usually bushy with a spreading or rounded crown of spiny intertwining branches and twigs, is a traditional component of hedgerows and thus forms so much a part of the British landscape. It is often called white thorn, or 'quick' – the old word for living, because it contrasted with the dead material used in earlier hedges and fences.

The zigzag shoots, except for some vigorous first-year ones, are armed with numerous short spines. Along the shoots, which are dull red above and green below, are set alternately very small reddish-black winter buds with many scales. The small dull green leaves are variable in size and shape, with three to seven lobes usually cut more than half way towards the midrib. The margins of the lobes are either undivided or bear a few teeth towards their apex. The stipules, large on vigorous shoots, soon fall.

Each inflorescence comprises up to about fifteen heavily scented bi-sexual flowers, with petals which are usually white, but occasionally pink. The tree begins to bloom properly in May, hence its common alternative name of 'May'. The small round fruit (the 'haw') changes in early September from green to scarlet. It retains the withered style from the flower, and there is very rarely more than one nutlet within the fleshy edible coat.

When young the bark is smooth, and greenish-grey or greenish-brown. Gradually it becomes a darker grey and gets rather rugged. It is often strongly fluted. The sapwood is white, and the heartwood a rust-brown. Being small in size, the timber is not of much account, but it was once favoured for wood-engravers' blocks, mallet-heads and tool handles.

12

Euonymus europaeus L. **Spindle Tree** CELASTRACEAE

Deciduous Native

Spindle Tree is small but interesting, and appears as a shrub particularly on the chalk downs, and locally on lime-rich soils. It is scarcely noticed before autumn, when the displays of its pretty fuchsia-pink seed-pods are conspicuous, accompanied by a delightful show of leaf colour, the green leaves changing to russet-red hues before they fall.

The young twigs are green (in autumn a conspicuous component of an otherwise brown hedgerow) and after the first year are four-angled, later developing pale brown cork ribs along the angles of the square; eventually they grow quite round. The winter buds are in opposite pairs. The leaves vary from oval to lance-shaped, with a finely toothed margin and a pointed tip. From a shining blue-mid-green (paler on the underside) they fade in autumn to yellow, russet and crimson.

The small greenish-white flowers are borne in June in loose clusters in the leaf axils. The trees are often either male or female though flowers including both sexes do occur on the same tree. The female flower produces a four-lobed seed-pod which is pale green at first, but changes to a vivid pink by October. Within a month or two the seed-pod splits open to expose the four bright orange pulpy coats (an aril) which each enclose a hard white seed within a pink seed-coat. The seeds are poisonous.

The bark is smooth, greenish at first, later becoming grey to pale brown. The hardness, smoothness and toughness of the whitish wood led to its early use for the spindles used for spinning wool by hand – explaining the tree's name. The wood also yields a fine charcoal for artists' use.

Spindle Tree is unpopular with farmers because it is an alternative host to the bean-fly.

13

Fagus sylvatica L. **Beech** FAGACEAE

Deciduous Native

Beech, one of Britain's best known trees, is seen particularly on chalk and limestone formations such as the Cotswolds, Chilterns and Downs. It is a graceful tall tree, sometimes called 'the Lady of the Woods'. The thick shade which it sheds usually keeps the forest floor bereft of undergrowth. The mature, almost mono-culture beechwood, has a beauty rarely surpassed.

The new shoots, grey and transparent, develop into long, thin, zig-zag twigs which hold pale brown winter buds, set alternately, and long and slender, with papery scales. The leaves are a tender pale green when opening in April, later becoming a rich deep green shade. They are oval, end in a short point, and have a wavy margin which with the veins on the underside and the leaf-stalks are at first hairy. In autumn the leaves change to glorious tints of bronze, orange and gold. Trees below a height of about 10 feet retain their spent red-brown leaves throughout winter, but larger trees strew them over the forest floor until they are swept by the wind to lie in deep drifts.

The male catkins are borne in groups of two or three soon after the leaves open; each catkin has a long thin drooping stalk which bears two or three slender scale leaves and ends in a tassel of about fifteen greenish flowers. The female catkins are small, green, and lie close to the stem. At first the fruit is an egg-shaped pointed green husk, clad in soft green hairs. In the autumn the husks turn brown, and after splitting into four lobes to release one or two triangular, smooth shining brown seeds ('beech nuts'), they often persist on the tree until the following spring. Good 'mast years' occur infrequently. The nuts provide, with acorns, pannage for pigs.

The thin bark is of a typical bright silver-grey or metallic colour, and remains smooth throughout the tree's life. In some parts of the country the naked circular columnar trunks have in part almost a purplish sheen. In outline Beech is large, upright, with a crown comprising a spreading network of fine branches. Its base is almost always buttressed. The wood is hard and strong, of a bright buff colour with mid-brown flecks ('pith rays'). Among its chief uses are furniture and turnery goods such as tool handles, bowls and spoons.

Beech freely regenerates from fallen seed It is usually planted pure, or as groups in a matrix of other trees, or as an underplant. It has a high amenity value.

Beeches with coppery red or deep purple foliage are frequently seen. The Copper Beech, variety *purpurea* (*atropunicea*), is a natural 'sport' discovered in the eighteenth century. The rich purplish-brown colour of its leaves masks their green chlorophyll within, but they function normally. The tree is usually grafted onto stock of the common Beech but will also grow from seed.

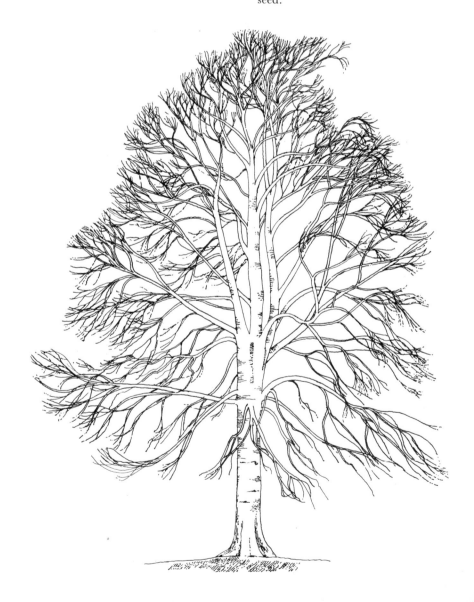

14

Fraxinus excelsior L. **Ash** OLEACEAE

Deciduous Native

Ash is among the most widely distributed of Britain's broad-leaved trees. It is the last native tree to come into leaf (mid-May) and the first to become bereft of foliage in autumn, though its fruits ('bunches of keys') often persist in large numbers throughout the winter.

The greenish-grey twigs are in pairs, and are knobbly because of the swollen leaf-scars. The prominent large black winter buds are oppositely set. So, too, are its compound-pinnate leaves, 6–9 inches long, comprising seven to fifteen leaflets with serrated margins, and channelled leaf-stalk.

The flowers, which appear well before the leaves, are purple, short-stalked, and in dense, almost knobbly clusters, the precocious flowering giving a purplish tinge to the whole crown. Some trees are male, and some female; some trees carry both sexes. The winged fruiting strap-shaped 'keys', likewise in clusters, each contain a seed at the base. When planted green they will germinate, but if allowed to become ripe and brown on the tree (usually by August) they remain in clusters throughout the winter, appearing in silhouette as hanging bats or swarms of birds awaiting migration, until scattered by the March winds.

The grey-green bark is smooth and thin for some years, but eventually turns grey, roughens and fissures, diagonally or criss-crossed, into a regular pattern. The tree grows tall and slender, with an open rounded crown. It has a tendency to fork, generally due to frost, but occasionally to the ash bud moth, destroying the terminal bud.

Ash likes alkaline soils, where it regenerates freely from fallen seed. Silviculturists prefer to plant it on deep rich soils, away from frost pockets. Its wood, yellowish or greyish-white with sometimes a pale brown heartwood, is tough, elastic and cleaves easily. Among its important uses are sports goods (tennis-racket frames, billiard cues and hockey sticks), oars, bar-hurdles, tent pegs, tool handles and furniture. It burns well – 'ash wet or ash dry, is fit for a Queen to warm her slippers by'. It is not a good hedgerow tree, being a 'robber' of adjacent soils on farmland.

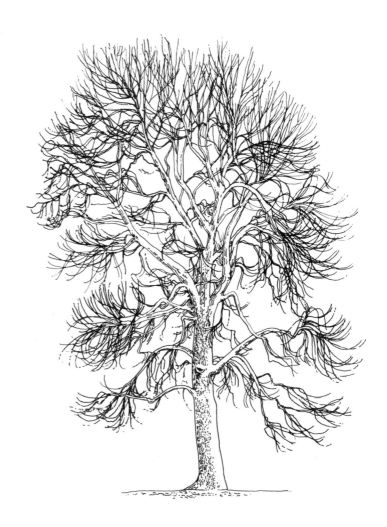

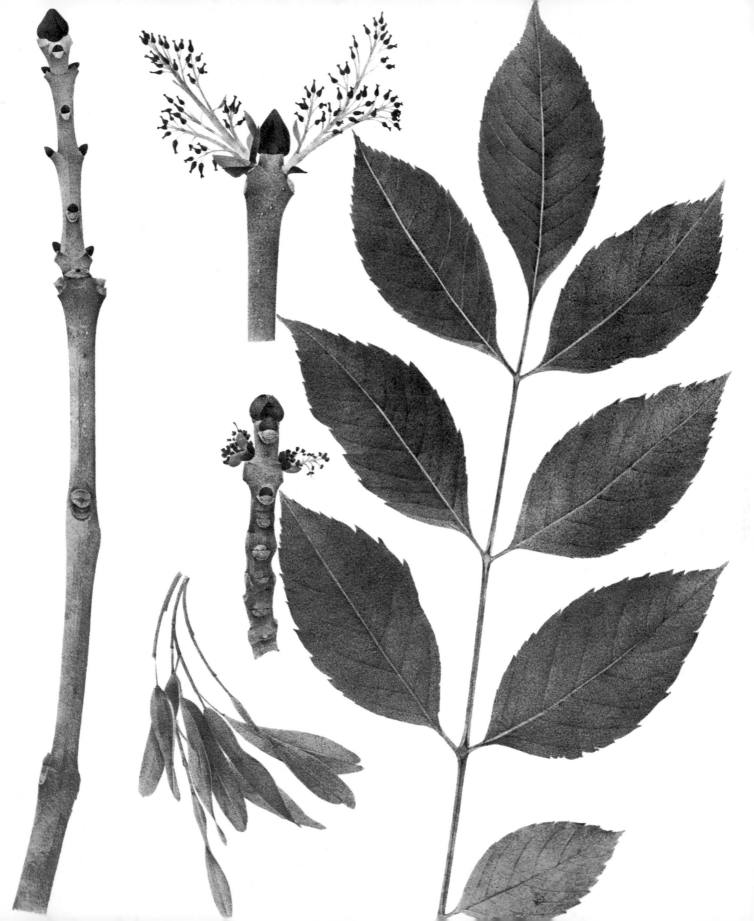

15

Ilex aquifolium L. **Holly** AQUIFOLIACEAE

Evergreen Native

Holly is probably Britain's best known tree – since ancient times it has been connected with pre-Christian festival and Christmas decoration. However, it is only locally common, mainly in hedgerows or scattered throughout older traditional forests. It is one of the smaller trees, although some specimens attain a height of 50 feet or even more. It will tolerate shade.

The twigs are stout, bright green or purplish, and slightly angled. The small winter buds are green and sharply pointed. The ovate leaves are dark green above and pale green below, with a waxy or varnished surface, and have a tough, leathery texture. Usually each leaf on the lower branches has a series of sharp points along its margin; higher up, each leaf has but a single point, right at the tip.

Very occasionally both sexes of flowers are found on one tree. Those trees with only male flowers, of course never berry. The small sweetly scented flowers of May and June are waxy white, lie in clusters in the leaf axils, and have all their parts in fours. The male has four stamens and no pistil. The female has a four-lobed ovary surmounted by a four-parted style and stigma, and rudimentary anthers. The well known decorative berries, green at first and later crimson, contain three or more hard black seeds.

The bark is smooth and grey to greenish-grey. Over its surface a darker network soon develops, and the bark gets somewhat rough and gnarled. The wood is ivory-white, and of a fine even texture, hard and heavy. It is well suited to turnery, inlaid work and carving. The tree is a useful hedgeplant, since it is evergreen and stands clipping well.

The many decorative garden kinds of holly include trees with variegated leaves, smooth leaves only, and yellow berries. The yellow-berried form is sometimes found growing wild.

16

Juglans regia L. **Walnut** JUGLANDACEAE

Deciduous

Walnut, usually found as a solitary specimen (and only rarely in woods), is best known for its nuts, its attractive grey (and valuable) trunk, and its exceptionally large compound-pinnate leaves. It was brought from Asia Minor or the Balkans in classical times, probably by the Romans. The name is derived from the Old English *wealh*, foreign.

The young shoots are stout, with large leaf scars and a laminated (layered) pith, and in colour are grey-green, later becoming greenish-bronze or grey. The winter buds, set alternately, are deep purple to black, velvety, with distinct, large horseshoe-shaped leaf scars. The compound-pinnate, long-stemmed leaves are at first bronze or purple-coloured, later becoming dull green on top, paler green underneath. The number of paired leaflets varies from two to six pairs (usually three to four), with a terminal leaflet which is generally the largest on the leaf. Usually the leaflets' margins are unbroken and wavy. When crushed, the leaves are strongly aromatic, and the juice stains the hand.

Both sexes of flower appear on the same tree, but separately, in early May. The males are in pendent curved catkins, green in colour at first but purplish when ready to shed their pollen. The females are in erect, few-flowered sessile clusters of about three. The plum-shaped fruit quickly swells, is green at first, becoming brown, and splitting irregularly to disclose the hard brown thin-shelled nut, wherein lies its edible crinkled kernel.

On young trees the bark is greyish-gree or greyish-red, and smooth, later broken shallow fissures into irregular flat-surface somewhat diamond-shaped ridges. The sa wood is broad and pale greyish-brown, while the heartwood is rich greyish-brow to chocolate colour but may have other tints, and is handsomely marked. It is heavy, hard and fine-textured, greatly valued for gunstocks, furniture, tablewar and interior decoration, being usually ap plied as a veneer.

The less common Black Walnut, *J. nig* L., is so called from the timber, which is a dark, purplish-brown colour. It is disti guished from the common Walnut by its reddish-brown twigs, which are downy, smooth; by the greater number of leaflet and their regularly serrated margins; an by the extremely hard-shelled casing, covered by a deeply chiselled pattern, wh encloses the barely edible nut. It grows into a much bigger and taller tree, with bl or dark brown, vertically fissured bark.

17

Malus sylvestris Mill. **Crab Apple** ROSACEAE

Deciduous Native

The common wild apple or Crab is a bushy, dense and much branched tree which may be found in untended woods or elsewhere throughout Britain. Though no one plants this tree, its blossom alone makes it worthwhile.

The interlacing branches bear long shoots that extend the framework of the crown, short shoots or 'spurs' that carry blossom, and sometimes shoots of medium length that are modified into sharp spines. The small winter buds are alternate and pointed, and have hairy scales. The bright green leaves are simple and oval, 1–2 inches long, with a toothed margin and a bluntly pointed tip.

The bi-sexual flowers which open late in April are usually pink in bud, becoming white or slightly flushed with pink when open. When ripe in autumn the fruit (a 'pome') is yellowish-green flushed with brownish-red, and about an inch in diameter; though very sour, it can be gathered to make the best sort of crab-apple jelly.

The bark is greyish-brown, and when old becomes furrowed, and peels off in thin flakes. The wood, red-brown and tough, has been often used for mallet heads and ornamental carving.

18

Platanus × *hispanica* Muenchh.; (*P.* × *acerifolia* Willd.) **London Plane** PLATANACEAE

Deciduous

London Plane is now generally accepted as being a hybrid between *P. occidentalis* and *P. orientalis,* probably originating in the mid seventeenth century. It is well known as a stately, tall, hardy and vigorous street tree with peeling bark, knobbly trunk and curved or crooked branches. In summer its broad leaves cast a gaily dappled shade, and the tree withstands lopping, and tolerates impure atmospheres.

The shoots are stout and brown, with alternate winter buds which are reddish and covered by a single closed scale. The leathery leaves are set alternately. On opening they are khaki colour, but later they are glossy green on top, paler underneath. They are palmately veined, usually with five lobes and have stipules united to form a long tube-like stalk.

The globular flower heads ('bobbles' or seed balls) dangle on long stalks in June, male and female being separate but on the same tree. The minute individual stalkless green flowers radiate from a central base. The developed fruits are clustered to form ball, about three-quarters of an inch in diameter, spiky with the remains of the styles. These brown 'bobbles' remain dangling on the otherwise bare tree throughout the winter, and break up in the following spring, releasing the individual fruit which resembles a tiny four-sided club, with the style projecting from the top and a parachute-like ring of hairs attached to the bottom.

The bark is thin and smooth, light greenish or yellowish-green in colour, and flakes off annually in irregular plates, particularly during late summer, to disclose much paler inner bark of green, yellow, and brown. When the tree is very big, the bark becomes dark grey and finely fissured. The flaking gives the trunk a dappled or mottled appearance, not unlike the colouring of a giraffe. The wood is pinkish-brown in colour, without any distinct heartwood. It is a useful veneer timber, and when quartered is often called 'lacewood'. The tree is very rarely planted commercially. Propagation is by seeds, cuttings, or by layering.

19

Populus alba L. **White Poplar, Abele** SALICACEAE

Deciduous

White Poplar is an attractive ornamental tree, handsome by reason of its pale bark and the glistening undersides of its quivering leaves. It was introduced in about 1548, and an old English name is 'abele', evolved from the Latin *alba*, white.

The young round shoots are at first white from their dense covering of matted, woolly down. The winter buds are covered likewise. The leaves on the short shoots are small and variable in shape, the margins being dentate or shallowly lobed and having a few blunt, more or less triangular teeth. Most of these early leaves are as broad as, or even broader than, their length, and the upper surface is deep green, and somewhat hairy; the lower surface is at first white from the thick down, but soon becomes grey. The even more downy leaves on the long summer shoots and suckers are larger, up to 4 inches across, and palmately lobed, with the lobes bearing a few bluntly triangular teeth. The leaf-stalks on all the leaves are round or slightly flattened, and downy.

The male pendent catkins, which open in early May, are some 2 or 3 inches long and have crimson anthers; the female catkins are rather shorter. Male and female trees are rarely found together, so fertile seed is seldom produced. Cuttings and suckers are the best means of propagation.

The attractive smooth and greyish-white bark has a greenish tinge and only slowly becomes black and roughened at the base. The tree is of no economic value, but many people appreciate its decorative attractions, particularly its silvery appearance in spring and the contrast of the white and golden leaves in autumn. It is a good seaside tree.

White Poplar is much confused with the possibly native Grey Poplar, *P. canescens* Sm., which grows faster, has a better shape, and reaches a larger size.

20

Populus nigra L. **Black Poplar** SALICACEAE

Deciduous Native

This poplar is native to Britain, though it is not common, and its epithet 'black' may have arisen only from contrast with the White Poplar (Pl. 19) and the Grey Poplar. It is a large heavily limbed tree, sparsely branched, with some of the main branches descending in arches. On its short massive trunk it often carries conspicuous large burrs.

The green shoots soon become yellow-ochre coloured, thereafter turning grey, and finally darkening. The oval winter buds are reddish and pointed, and are set at uneven intervals on all sides of the twigs. The leaves are triangular to rhombic in shape, though the basal angles are rounded, not sharp. They open as khaki or light brown, but are soon deep green on top, paler underneath, with a translucent margin which bears shallow teeth. The long stalks are flattened close to the leaf-blade. The leaves turn yellow in autumn.

The attractive male catkins expand and hang like lambs' tails in March before the leaves unfold; the anthers are crimson until they show their pale yellow pollen. The female catkins, never on the same tree as the male, are longer, with stout greenish-white stigmas. They fall in early June as numerous small down-clad capsules but they seldom contain seed. The tree is propagated by cuttings. It rarely produces suckers.

The bark is almost black, deeply and irregularly furrowed into broad, thick ridges. The wood is almost white in colour, soft and light, very open in texture but with woolly fibres. It is used for packing cases, and general purposes.

Black Poplar has now been replaced for commercial planting by its quicker-growing hybrid clones, such as *Populus* 'Serotina'. These are established on fertile, well-watered lowland soils to yield timber for match sticks, match boxes and baskets.

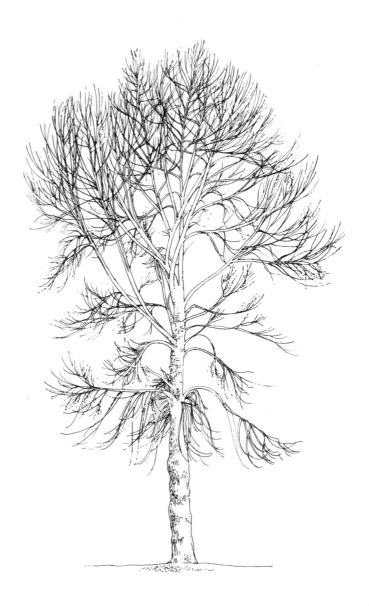

21

Populus nigra 'Italica' du Roi **Lombardy Poplar** SALICACEAE

Deciduous

Lombardy Poplar is Britain's best known poplar, being a narrow erect tall tree with a graceful plume-like fastigiate outline which adds dignity to the landscape. It was introduced from Italy in about 1758. The male sex is common in Britain; the female less common.

The green shoots become pale yellow, then greyish or brown. The reddish-brown winter buds are oval and pointed. The leaves are triangular in shape, though the basal angles are rounded, not sharp.

The short pendent male catkins have red anthers. They shed pollen in late March or early April. Female catkins are longer, green and curved.

The bark soon becomes rugged, and is almost black at the base, smooth and grey or brown on the upper part. The branches are all more or less erect. The tree normally never suckers, but when cut down suckers arise over practically the whole extent covered by its root system. It is useless for timber particularly on account of its numerous knots. The main purpose of planting the tree is to provide a screen, or a barrier against wind, dust and noise. It is easily struck from cuttings.

22

Populus tremula L. **Aspen** SALICACEAE

Deciduous Native

Aspen, a moderate-sized poplar, erect with a slender crown and trunk, is perhaps best known from its roundish leaves which almost ceaselessly quiver and rustle even on calm days. It is very hardy and tolerates wet places; unfortunately perhaps, it is often surrounded with numerous suckers which may even form a thicket.

The young green shoots soon become smooth and golden brown, and then darken. The branchlets are smooth and shiny with winter buds that are shiny reddish-brown and sometimes somewhat sticky. The roundish leaves, on a long thin much flattened leaf-stalk, are dull, rich green on top, paler yellow underneath; three prominent veins radiate from the base, and the outer rim has indented edges and is sometimes tinged with red. The quivering leaves persist on the tree late into the autumn, turning a rich yellow before they fall.

The male catkins, which open late in February, are woolly on account of the deeply cut and hairy scales; they have purple stamens, later contrasting with the yellow pollen. The female flowers are at first green; when they fall they strew the ground with white down. The seed capsules burst in the latter part of May, but seed rarely germinates well. Propagation is best by root cuttings

At first the bark is pale greenish-grey and smooth, becoming dark grey and rugged with age. The white wood is light and soft, and is excellent for match sticks and match boxes. Other uses include 'chip' baskets, paper pulp and wood wool. The tree seldom reaches a suitable timber size in Britain, so attempts to cultivate it are rare.

23

Prunus avium L. **Wild Cherry, Gean** ROSACEAE

Deciduous Native

The common Wild Cherry or Gean, is to be found sparingly in mixed woodlands as a moderate-sized tree, or occasionally as a tall tree of open habit, the lower branches spreading but the remainder ascending steeply.

The twigs are greyish-brown, and the winter buds are alternate, brown, and pointed on short spur shoots. The pale green, 2–3 inch long elliptical leaves, which droop somewhat on fairly long stalks, have finely toothed margins, and are without hairs on the upper surface, but downy below. They turn brilliant crimson in autumn.

The white, sweetly scented, bi-sexual, self-sterile flowers, with long, slender stalks, are cup-shaped and borne in clusters (umbels) of from two to six in April-May. The fruit (a cherry) is small and shiny, changing from green through bright red to purple when ripe in July; the taste is sweet or bitter, never acid.

The bark is grey or reddish-brown, smooth and shiny, ringed with orange-coloured lenticels, and peels horizontally in thin strips. In older trees the lower bark becomes rough and furrowed. The attractive wood is golden or even greenish-brown, rather heavy, tough and hard. It is a good furniture timber, and is prized as a turnery wood for such items as bowls.

Foresters value Gean as an amenity tree, particularly on the edges of plantations. It suckers freely, and it coppices when cut.

24

Prunus padus L. **Bird Cherry** ROSACEAE

Deciduous Native

This small slender cherry tree, sometimes only a bush, is particularly at home along stream sides in the Scottish Highlands, but is rarely found in the south of England and infrequently in northern England, Wales and its borders. The crown is rounded, the upper branches ascending steeply, the lower spreading and even drooping.

The winter buds are stout, shiny, sharply pointed, and often bent; their scales vary in colour from yellow to dark brown. The young shoots turn olive-green and eventually dark brown. The 2–3 inch long leaves are elliptical with finely toothed margins, and are dull green on top and pale green below.

There are up to forty small, white, bisexual, self-fertile flowers, which open in May, in each drooping or spreading spike-like raceme. The fruit (a cherry) changes from green to black, is shiny, up to half an inch in diameter, and harsh and bitter to the taste; it ripens in August, and is relished by birds.

The bark is dark brown, and remains smooth, but is not shiny. The bands of orange-coloured lenticels are much shorter than those on Gean (Pl. 23). The bark peels, and like the sappy wood has an unpleasant smell of bitter almonds. The sapwood is white, and the heartwood dark purplish-brown.

Bird Cherry seems to spread more by suckering than from seed, though seedlings are extremely hardy and easily raised. It has produced several varieties and distinct geographical forms but as found growing wild in Britain does not vary greatly.

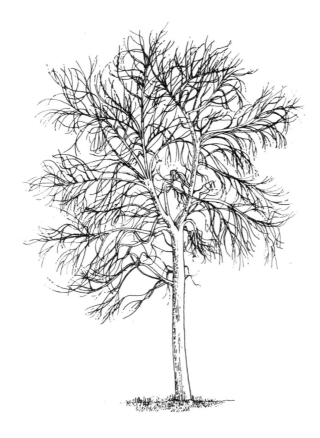

25

Prunus spinosa L. **Blackthorn, Sloe** ROSACEAE

Deciduous Native

Blackthorn, commonly called Sloe, is a dwarfish tree which grows abundantly in hedgerows where, because of its many suckers and vicious black thorns, it is unpopular with farmers, or on waste ground often forming impenetrable dense thickets.

Its black, thorn-studded twigs carry small alternate winter buds that are oval, bluntly pointed, and reddish to purplish-black in colour. The small (about an inch long) oval leaves are tender green on opening, have pointed tips, shallowly toothed margins, and dull red stalks. The leaves later become longer and narrower, and a much darker duller green.

The leaves are usually preceded (though sometimes followed) in April by clouds of small, star-shaped, white, bi-sexual blossoms. The small round fruit ('sloe') ripens through green to a lustrous purplish-black that has a smooth bluish-white waxy bloom. The pale green flesh is intensely bitter to the taste, and the stone is brown. The fruits are the source of sloe jelly. They are often fermented to produce sloe wine and if pickled in spirit they provide sloe gin.

The bark is black and on old trees it becomes broken into small square plates. The sapwood is pale yellow, and the heartwood dark brown and tough. Though the tree is too small for use as timber, knobbly walking sticks are made from it, and the wood was used to make the traditional Irish shillelagh.

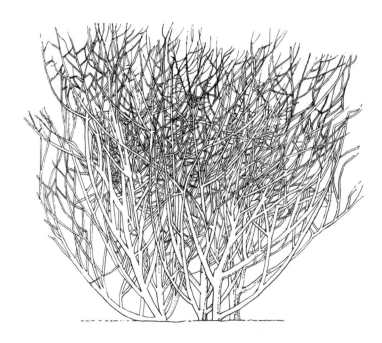

26

Quercus cerris L. **Turkey Oak** FAGACEAE

Deciduous

Turkey Oak, a wide-crowned tree with ascending lanky limbs and branches, deeply lobed leaves, mossy-cupped acorns, and curious bark, was introduced to Britain probably from the Balkans, in 1735.

The twigs are brown, with a knobbly look, and carry spiral, alternate, brown winter buds which are small and downy, almost hidden by the long persistent stipules. The leaves vary in size and in their deep and saw-tooth-like lobes. Their upper surface is dull green, the lower much paler in colour. They persist on the trees later than those on Britain's native oaks.

The flowers of both sexes appear on the same tree in May. The long pendent tassel-like male catkins are greenish-yellow; so too are the short-stalked female flowers. The acorn, with its mossy-covered, rather shallow cup, takes two years in which to ripen.

The bark is rough, dark grey and fissured. A distinct swelling occurs both at the junction of the ascending branches with the trunk, and on the twigs. The wood, though heavy, is prone to warping and shrinkage; few merchants will purchase it, thus reducing its use to little but firewood. This inferiority is unfortunate, because the tree grows faster and straighter than all Britain's other hardwoods except poplar, willow and ash.

In 1765 a remarkable hybrid between Turkey Oak and the Cork Oak, *Q. suber* L., was raised by an Exeter nurseryman named Lucombe. This Lucombe Oak, *Q.* × *hispanica* 'Lucombeana', forms a magnificent park tree, with leaves like the Turkey Oak but dark green above and also more or less evergreen; some have a grey, corky bark.

27

Quercus ilex L. **Holm** or **Evergreen Oak** FAGACEAE

Evergreen

Holm Oak, Britain's only common evergreen oak, was introduced during the sixteenth century from the Mediterranean. It is a moderate sized tree with a broad, rounded, dense crown and leaves which are usually almost oval and never lobed. The tree is common in gardens and parks, where it stands like a large holly, often drooping almost to the ground and casting a dense shade throughout the whole year.

The young shoots are grey-green, carrying small, downy winter buds. The oval or linear leaves, which are usually 1–2 inches long but vary greatly in size and shape, have a margin which is shallowly toothed or even without teeth, and although rather woolly in May, they become dark green and hairless on top, but greyish- or yellowish-green underneath on account of the short, thick down.

The flowers of both sexes appear on the same tree in May. The greenish-yellow male catkins vary in length and are borne in abundance; the female flowers, of like colour, have a longish stalk. The acorn is short, and at least half of it is enclosed in a downy cup; both are green at first, becoming dark brown when ripe (which takes two years).

The bark is grey, later becoming brown or nearly black, and divided into fairly small squares. The wood is hard, heavy, tough, and highly figured, but rarely used.

The tree may not be attractive, but often provides a useful screen and shelter from sun and wind. It is particularly useful by the sea because it gives shade and shelter, and it resists the ill effects of salt laden winds and also atmospheric pollution in towns.

28

Quercus petraea Lieb. **Sessile** or **Durmast Oak** FAGACEAE

Deciduous Native

The Sessile or Durmast Oak, one of Britain's two native oaks, is particularly differentiated from the Pedunculate Oak (Pl. 29) in having long-stalked leaves, stalkless acorn cups, straighter branches, and a narrower crown.

The twigs are brown and carry brown winter buds spirally set, with a cluster of them near the tip. The young shoots bear hairy scales. The leaves are often bronze to khaki when opening, and later are sometimes tinged with red – especially the second growth in July. They have a wavy indented outline, vary in size and lobing, and have an appreciable stalk towards which the base of the leaf tapers gradually. Unlike the Pedunculate Oak, it does not have auricles.

Both sexes of flowers appear on the same tree in May. The pale green male catkins are slender; the even less conspicuous female flowers, of like colour, are in twos and threes, and have little or no stalks – hence the later cup which holds the acorn likewise does not have a stalk. Both the acorn and the cup are at first green, but become brown by autumn.

The bark, trunk and wood characteristics are the same as those of the Pedunculate Oak but the tree has usually a better timber form, since it keeps a main trunk growing up through its crown of straight branches. Young trees up to about 10 feet retain their spent brown autumn leaves until the new green ones appear in the spring.

The comments made in the last two paragraphs under Pedunculate Oak apply equally to the Sessile Oak.

29

Quercus robur L. **Pedunculate** or **English Oak** FAGACEAE

Deciduous Native

Oak, by long tradition, is the national tree of England, being associated with her shipbuilding and hence with her 'wooden walls'. Its acorns ('mast') provided, with beech nuts, pannage for pigs, and its bark yielded tannin for leather. Of Britain's two native oaks, the English or Pedunculate is more rugged than the Sessile or Durmast (Pl. 28), and has leaves on short stalks, with the acorn cups on long stalks whereas the Durmast has long-stalked leaves and stalkless acorn cups.

The twigs of Pedunculate Oak are grey-brown and carry light brown winter buds spirally set, with a cluster of them near the tip. The young shoots bear very little down; and the bud-scales are not downy. The leaves are often bronze to khaki when opening, and later are sometimes tinged with red – especially the second growth in July. They have a wavy indented outline, vary in size and lobing, and have a short stalk, on either side of which the leaf usually forms two ear-like lobes called auricles.

Both sexes of flower appear on the same tree in May. The pale green male catkins are slender; the much less conspicuous female flowers, of like colour, have appreciable stalks – hence the later cup which holds the acorn likewise has a stalk. Both the acorn and the cup are at first green, but become brown by autumn.

At first the bark is smooth and greyish-brown, later becoming rugged, giving a rough fissured grey trunk that is often buttressed and sometimes carries epicormic shoots. In some parts of the country the trunks have in part almost a dull pink to purplish sheen. The sapwood band is white while the heartwood is rich golden brown, and has great strength and remarkable natural durability. The timber has a wide range of uses, from cleft or sawn fencing and gates to furniture and parts of buildings, also shipbuilding, particularly Scottish fishing craft; the bark can be used for tanning leather. The tree has a typically widely spaced and much branched crown. Young trees up to about 10 feet retain their spent brown autumn leaves until the new green ones appear in the spring.

The 'oak-apple' (illustrated) is formed by a minute gall wasp.

Silviculturists might say that whereas oak has had a glorious past, its economic future is less certain because of its slow growth relative to conifers, yet trees of sixty years can attain 60 feet in height and 8 feet in girth. It is sometimes said of the oak that it is two hundred years growing, two hundred years standing still and two hundred years dying. The silviculturist would usually fell it between one hundred and two hundred years.

The Pedunculate Oak and the Sessile Oak (which it has largely replaced) have sometimes interbred, and many oakwoods consist of intermediate forms. Though little attention is given to differentiating between the two timbers, records show that many woodmen have appreciated the difference. Both kinds of tree usually break bud in May, but there is a second period of growth in July or August, when the so-called Lammas shoots are produced.

30

Quercus rubra L. sec. du Roi, (*Q. borealis* Mich.) **Red Oak** FAGACEAE

Deciduous

Red Oak, a graceful round-headed tree with light grey bark, is one of the several North American red oaks which have been planted in Britain as an amenity tree on account of the beauty of its autumn foliage. More recently it has been planted experimentally for its timber.

The young shoots are rather stout, often five-sided, and olive-green to reddish-brown. The brown winter buds are alternately ar-ranged, but towards the tip of the twigs they form clusters. The leaves are larger than those of Britain's native oaks, and have sharply angled lobes. They vary in size and shape, and the vein of each lobe projects as a bristle beyond the point. At first the leaves are a pale yellow, later green, and in autumn they turn a dull to rich red-brown.

The flowers of both sexes appear on the same tree in May. The male catkins are yellowish-green, long, and sometimes very numerous; the female flowers are shortly stalked. The acorns, which do not mature until the second year, are dumpy and flat-based, standing in shallow cups.

The light grey bark remains smooth for long time. Only after many years does it develop a slightly rough surface. The wood is open textured, with large pores, and lack the strength and durability of the native oaks. It will probably be used for cheaper furniture and flooring. The tree grows fast even on soils of moderate fertility, and pla a small role in British forestry.

31

Salix caprea L. **Goat Willow, Sallow** SALICACEAE

Deciduous Native

Goat Willow (so called because goats readily browse it) is a pleasant small tree, well known for the early appearance in spring of its silver (female) or golden (male) catkins or 'palm', followed by oval, not slender, leaves. Other names for it are Sallow and Pussy Willow.

The twigs are smooth and reddish-brown, and carry round yellow-green winter buds concealed in a single scale which becomes weather-reddened towards the top. The oval leaves, 1–2 inches long, have a wavy margin and a pointed tip. They are lighter and hairy on the underside, and have two prominent stipules - little leaflets – at the base of the stalk.

The sexes are never on the same tree. The female catkins begin to appear in January or February as attractive silvery-downy flower heads. The erect male catkins have showy golden anthers which open in March. The seeds are small and hairy.

The bark is smooth, greenish-brown at first, becoming dark brown on older trees. The wood is pale cream to pinkish-brown, and woolly, but it is rarely used. Like other willows, Sallow coppices with much vigour. It is a very pretty component of mixed broad-leaved woodland, and of some usefulness as a natural pioneer species, being able to establish itself on all types of waste ground.

32

Salix fragilis L. **Crack Willow** SALICACEAE

Deciduous Native

Crack Willow, one of Britain's many willows, is common by watersides, in marshes, and in wet, open woods. Often it is found treated as a pollard; otherwise it usually rises some 30–60 feet and often more, as a spreading bright green foliaged tree. The name arises from the sharp crack which is made when twigs are easily snapped off just by their junction with the branch.

The twigs are smooth, and olive-green or brown in colour. The alternate winter buds are brown, slender, pointed, enclosed in a single scale, and appressed. The leaves are slender, 3–6 inches long, serrated on the margin, bright green on the upper surface, paler or glaucous underneath.

The erect catkins open in May, the sexes always on different trees. The male catkins are about 2 inches long, and have golden anthers; the females are longer and more slender. The hairy seed is released when the capsule valves split.

At first the green bark is smooth, becoming rough and grey when older. The wood is pale cream to pinkish-brown, soft and brittle, so is seldom used. The poles grown on pollards provide stakes. This willow is very easily grown from dormant shoots.

The White Willow, *S. alba* L., is distinguished particularly by its silvery leaves and its tower-like form. The Cricket Bat Willow, *S.* × *coerulea* Sm., is a hybrid between *alba* and *fragilis*.

33

Sambucus nigra L. **Elder** CAPRIFOLIACEAE

Deciduous Native

Elder grows wild almost everywhere in Britain. Usually it is no more than a bush, but it can form a small tree.

The twigs are stout but brittle, since they hold a thick white pith. They are often angular and bear vertical corky pores on their bark. The buds are oppositely set, with a clear leaf scar below them, and several loose brownish-red or purple scales. The leaves are compound-pinnate, comprised of five to seven oval leaflets with toothed margins, somewhat resembling Ash.

The fragrant, bi-sexual creamy-white June blossoms stand above the foliage in flat-topped cymes of 5-6 inches diameter. These blossoms are sometimes brewed to make a refreshing or medicinal tea. The flowers are succeeded by small green globular berries, eventually juicy and purple-black, much used for the making of elderberry wine.

On young stems the bark is pale yellowish-brown, with prominent vertically disposed lenticels, which are at first pale but become darker. Later the bark rapidly becomes furrowed and corky, thick and greyish-brown in colour. The wood when old becomes hard and heavy; it is white, and horny in texture.

Elder is often treated as a weed, but sometimes as a favoured covert plant. In sheltered places it may carry some green leaf throughout most of the year, but a hard frost will blacken and cripple the foliage.

34

Sorbus aria L. **Whitebeam** ROSACEAE

Deciduous Native

Whitebeam is a rather small tree usually found on the fringes of woodlands, or in untended hedgerows or on crags. It is particularly at home on chalk and limestone soils, and is fairly common on the Cotswolds, the North Downs and the Chiltern Hills. It is probably best known for the conspicuous white underside of its leaves.

The young shoots soon become smooth and turn through reddish-brown to shiny and deep brown, and eventually grey, marked by numerous small, pale-coloured, wart-like lenticels. The twigs branch at an acute angle. The large greenish ovoid winter buds are pointed, with usually some brown or purple on the scales. The tree unfolds its leaves in pleasing erect cup-shaped groups, appearing glistening white due to a dense coating of white hairs on the exposed lower surfaces. When expanded, the leaves are oval, generally gently curved at both base and apex, and have many pairs of straight veins. The margin is toothed, and the upper surface, unlike the lower, is rather dull green and almost hairless. The faded pale grey leaves of autumn strew the floor below the tree, creating almost a mystic purplish-grey sheen.

The flat-topped inflorescence, which opens in May, has showy white bi-sexual flowers almost half an inch across, gathered into loose clusters. They are succeeded by almost round, dark green, hairy 'bloomed' fruits, which change to colours varying from orange-red to deep scarlet (usually the latter), the surface being marked by lenticels.

The bark is greenish-grey, and smooth except in old trees, when it becomes fissured and slaty-grey. The wood is yellowish-white, finely grained, fairly hard, heavy and strong, but is of little economic importance. The word 'beam' is the Saxon equivalent for tree.

An intermediate race, the Swedish Whitebeam, *S. intermedia*, has lobed leaves with toothed edges; it is common in north-east Scotland.

35

Sorbus aucuparia L. **Rowan, Mountain Ash** ROSACEAE

Deciduous Native

Rowan is one of Britain's most attractive small trees, usually seen as a solitary specimen throughout woodlands or scattered in rocky, mountainous regions. It is best known for its graceful slender outline, attractive feathery leaves, and gay bunches of white flowers in May, followed by a brilliant show of bright scarlet berries in September.

The shoots are downy at first but become smooth and greyish-brown. The spur shoots are stout and numerous, carrying dark brown buds, set alternately and covered with whitish down. The leaves are arranged alternately, compound-pinnate, with five to seven pairs of oval leaflets, and a terminal leaflet, each with a toothed margin. Their upper surface is deep green; the lower is grey-green; they turn bright shades of red and carmine in autumn.

The flat-topped inflorescence, a compound cyme, is comprised of numerous small creamy-white bi-sexual flowers, which open in late May. These are followed in July by green berries which during August and September turn orange and then bright scarlet. They are usually round (occasionally somewhat more barrel-shaped), and contain one or two small brown seeds. The berries have a high vitamin C content; though sour, they can be made into a tasty jelly.

The bark is smooth and grey, encircled by rings of lenticels. The tree is usually erect, but some older trees develop spreading crowns. The sapwood is yellow and the heartwood purplish-brown, hard and smooth, but is rarely sufficiently large to be utilised.

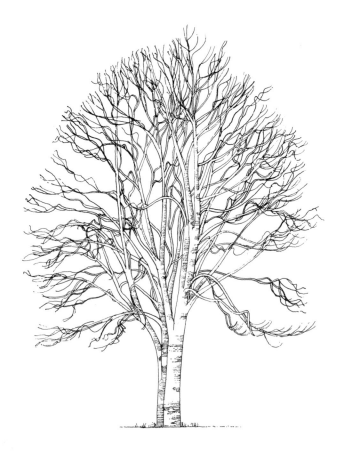

36

Sorbus torminalis L. **Wild Service Tree** ROSACEAE

Deciduous Native

Wild Service Tree, usually attaining between 30–50 feet in height, is very local, and one seldom finds more than a few trees growing in the same locality. The tree is particularly uncommon outside southern England and South Wales. It is curious because of its unusually shaped leaves, its flowers and fruits which resemble those of Rowan, and its bark which has the appearance of that of Hawthorn.

The winter buds are large, oval (not pointed), and greenish with brown edges to the scales. The young shoots soon become smooth and dark brown. The leaves are somewhat like Norway Maple but smaller, not pointed, and are coarsely toothed, borne alternately on the shoots, and not palmately veined. The lower pair of lobes is cut much more deeply than the others. The leaves are rather lustrous deep green on top, pale green or yellowish underneath. They turn yellow and crimson in autumn.

The flat-topped inflorescence, which opens in June, is comprised of small creamy-white bi-sexual flowers which are followed by green oval berries that later turn brown and drab, and become wrinkled and marked with numerous lenticels.

The bark is grey to black, smooth at first, later dividing into small thin scales which are shed. Suckers are produced. The wood is tough, and has a whitish sapwood and a red-brown heartwood.

It is uncertain to what extent this interesting and uncommon tree justifies its old name as a cure for colic (*tormina*); its berries are acid to the taste.

37

Tilia × *europaea* L. **Lime, Linden** TILIACEAE

Deciduous Native

Lime, one of Britain's tallest broadleaved trees, with oval crown, arching lower branches, and red twigs, is a well known and well-loved species, particularly in June and July when it is adorned with strongly scented yellowish flowers worked vigorously and noisily by honey-bees. For long it was a tree favoured for avenues, but more recently it is less appreciated because of its often fluted and wide-spreading base, bushy unsightly stems (including witches' brooms), and large bosses on its bole and base, from which may arise a mass of unwanted shoots.

The twigs are strongly zigzagged and reddish, dull crimson in colour. The winter buds are tinged with red, and have only two visible scales, one much larger than the other. The 2–3 inch long leaves have toothed margins, are heart-shaped, usually unequal at the base, and are dull green on the upper surface and pale green and rather shiny underneath – which underside is conspicuous when the foliage billows in the wind. Red or pink bud-scales are often associated with the leaves. The foliage is sometimes infested in midsummer with numerous tiny aphids, which exude sticky 'honey-dew'. The leaves turn yellow or golden in the early autumn.

The yellowish-green bi-sexual flowers are borne in June and July in clusters of four to ten on a long main stalk which also carries a narrowly oblong papery bract. Each flower has five green sepals and five greenish-white to yellow petals. The hard round downy seeds ripen in October.

At first the bark is smooth and greyish-green, striped with darker markings, but eventually becomes rough and fissured. It is fibrous and tough, and when young this 'bast' can be used for tying bundles of woodland produce. The wood is white, smooth, even-grained and soft, much used in the past, and still occasionally, by the wood sculptor, and for hat blocks and piano keys. If felled, Lime coppices vigorously. It tolerates lopping and trimming. The tree is rarely planted in woodlands.

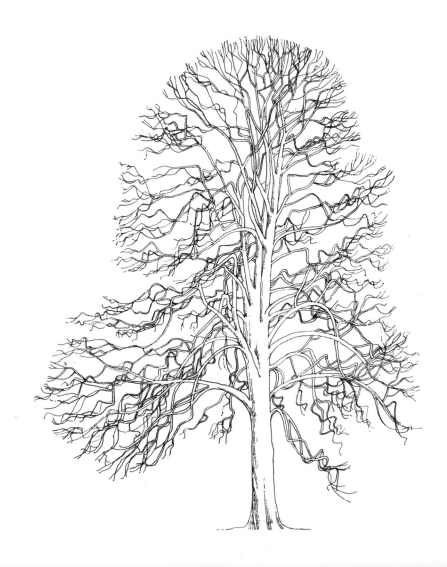

38

Ulmus glabra Huds. **Wych Elm** ULMACEAE

Deciduous Native

Wych Elm is quite a different tree from the English Elm (Pl. 39) found in hedgerows, being at home in the woods, though seldom if ever cultivated by foresters, and has a dome-like crown built around a forked trunk, with branches spreading and often pendulous towards their ends. Unlike English Elm, neither corky shoots nor suckers are normally present, and reproduction is by seed.

The brownish-grey twigs are stouter than those of the English Elm, and the young shoots grow practically at right angles to the branches. At first they are thickly covered by short hairs, but by their third year are smooth – hence the epithet *glabra*. The winter buds are chocolate brown, sharply pointed, with hairy scales. The leaves are larger than those of the English Elm, and have a shorter stalk. They are uneven at the base (asymmetrical), so that one side usually forms an 'ear' overlapping the stalk. The margins are sharply serrated, and the blade broadens towards the tip, and then suddenly narrows, the apex being drawn to a point. The upper surface is rough to the touch because of minute but harsh hairs.

The clusters of bi-sexual precocious flowers are purplish-crimson, and in mass give a reddish tinge to the whole crown when they appear on the leafless twigs during late February or March. The green transparent winged seeds (samaras) are somewhat larger than those of the English Elm. They are fully formed in about three weeks (again before the leaves) and ripen by May or early June. They cling festooned in masses of dense clusters until mid-June when they turn brown and then fall.

On young trees the bark is smooth and green. On older trees it is brown, thick and rough in more continuous ridges, more deeply furrowed than that of the English Elm and much more coarsely networked. The word 'wych' means supple, and the pliable strength of the wood has led to its use in boat and carriage-building, as shafts and tool handles, as well as for furniture.

39

Ulmus procera Salis. **English Elm** ULMACEAE

Deciduous Native

The English Elm, a tree found only in Britain, holds a traditional place in the lowland landscape because of its adaptability to life in hedgerows – due to its ability to spring up as sucker shoots from the roots of established trees. Unfortunately in recent years the Dutch Elm Disease has greatly reduced the numbers of this fine tree.

The young shoots branch from the stem at an angle of about 60° whereas in Wych Elm (Pl. 38) they are about 90°. The long shoots have a zigzag growth, and some are irregularly ridged with a corky substance – they are then called 'suberose'. The small winter buds are of a darker brown than the twigs; they are oval, end in a blunt point, and show several scales. The leaves are oval, with a much toothed margin and a short point; at the base they are oblique or uneven (asymmetrical), and the upper surface is roughened by short hairs. Patches of the foliage turn golden yellow in late summer, but the autumn leaves are among the latest of deciduous trees to fall.

The clusters of bi-sexual precocious flowers are purplish-crimson, and in mass give a reddish tinge to the whole crown when they appear during February or early March clustered close on the leafless twigs. The fruit, a seed (samara) is also formed before the leaves, and lies in the centre of a pale green oval wing which is transparent, and notched at the apex. The wings cling festooned in masses of dense green clusters until June when they turn brown and then fall. Fertile seeds are rarely produced in spite of the numerous fruits that develop. English Elm is therefore usually established by rooted suckers.

In outline the tree is usually tall, with two, three or four tiers of crown, and very rarely forked. The grey bark, smooth at first, becomes thick and furrowed into rather narrow ridges or dark grey-blackish squares. The trunk often carries burrs and tufts of epicormic shoots. The heartwood is reddish or dark brown, coarse-textured, strong, firm and heavy, usually with an interlocked grain – hence it is extremely difficult to split and has a tendency to warp. It is long lasting if kept either continuously dry or continuously wet. Among its uses are coffin boards, chairs, tables, cabinets, stools, underwater goods, and furniture for house and garden.

40

Viburnum opulus L. **Guelder Rose** CAPRIFOLIACEAE

Deciduous Native

Guelder Rose, a shrubby tree rarely exceeding 15 feet in height, delights the eye whenever adorned with its pretty clusters of curious white flowers or its very attractive scarlet translucent berries. It is common in the south of Britain, occasional in the Midlands, but very rare further north.

The twigs and branches are quite smooth, and somewhat angular, greenish-grey at first, later reddish-brown. The winter buds are set oppositely, greenish-yellow, and wrapped in scales. The opposite young leaves are covered with down when they appear, but they discard this as they expand into their deeply toothed lobes, usually three or five in number, with a few small glands down the stalk and a few reddish-brown stipules at its base.

The attractive flower-head, opening in June, has its individual flowers arranged as a flat-topped cyme, those in the outer circle being white and showy but sterile (without stamens or pistil), and those within being small, creamy white, bell-shaped and perfect – truly a curious but beautiful arrangement. The attractive flat clusters of scarlet translucent berries, nauseous to the taste, are often too heavy to be held up by their twigs, and branches become bent down under their weight. They ripen in autumn just as the leaves are fading to orange or russet tints.

41

Abies grandis Lindl. **Grand Fir** PINACEAE

Evergreen

Grand Fir, also commonly called by its botanical name of 'grandis,' is a tall rapidly-growing silver fir, introduced from the Pacific coast of North America in 1833, and re-introduced in 1855.

The new shoots are smooth and olive-green. The buds are small, blunt, and resin-coated. The needles are long (for firs), up to 2 inches, twisted at their base so as to spread in two ranks in one plane; the upper rank has the shorter needles. They have notched apices, and are glossy green above, with two prominent glaucous bands below. The new pale green needles, which appear in June, fringe the edges of all the branches, giving the tree its best appearance. When crushed, the scent is pleasantly aromatic. When pulled away from the stem they leave a neat round scar, not a peg.

Both sexes of flowers are found on the same tree. The small yellow male flowers are in clusters on the underside of the branches. The females are erect, short, scaly, and yellow-green, borne high up on the tree and are thus seldom seen. On fertilisation they develop into erect cylindrical cones up to 4 inches long and an inch or more broad, and slightly indented at the apex. They ripen to a yellowish-green, and disintegrate in September leaving the persistent central spike on the tree.

The bark is smooth, with some blisters containing clear, aromatic resin. With age the bark becomes dark-brown, fissured and scaly. The branches are in whorls, often wide apart. The wood is white or pale cream in colour, with no marked heartwood. It is used for box-making, paperpulp, and for general purposes where strength and natural durability are not required. Sometimes a 'drought crack' runs in spiral fashion up the stem.

Foresters prize 'grandis' as 'a fast and heavy volume-producer of moderately strong timber', and as a useful underplant. It can reach 130 feet in fifty years; and trees of 170 feet are known.

The European Silver Fir, *Abies alba* Mill., usually fails in Britain because of attacks by tiny needle-sucking aphids, species of *Adelges*. Consequently it is not planted here for timber, and but little for ornament.

42

Abies procera Rehd. **Noble Fir** PINACEAE

Evergreen

Noble Fir, a large and strikingly handsome conifer, is particularly distinguished by its glistening silvery green foliage and pale bluish-grey bark. It was introduced from Washington or Oregon in 1830.

The new shoots are rusty brown. The buds are small, round and resin-tipped. The needles are dense and upswept, massed on the top of the twig. They are a shining bluish-green on both surfaces, the upper being grooved. When pulled away they leave a neat round scar, not a peg.

Both sexes of flowers are found on the same tree. The handsome male catkins are deep purple, and borne in groups on the undersides of the lower shoots. The female flowers, reddish or yellowish-green with long bracts, are erect and are to be found near the top of the tree and are thus seldom seen (though some specimens flower when only 15–20 feet tall). These develop into decorative large erect cylindrical pale green cones, 6 inches or more long, and 3 inches or more wide, developing dark grey scales partly covered by long green, reflexed, feathery bracts. They become brown and ripen and disintegrate in September leaving the persistent central spike on the tree.

The bark is thin at first and pale grey, with some resin blisters. Later the bark is pale bluish or silver-grey, becoming broken by narrow grooves into irregular plates covered with scales that flake off to show a red inner bark. The stem bears whorls of branches, and often shows a marked taper, terminating in a stout leader that usually has to help to bear the weight of many heavy cones on its short side branches. The wood is brownish-white, somewhat similar to Spruce, and is used for joinery, packing cases, paper pulp, and general purposes.

The tree is doing well silviculturally, on a small scale, in damp, cold mountain situations in Wales and Scotland, where it has proved hardy and stands exposure well. It is a useful and attractive underplant.

43

Cedrus atlantica (Endl.) Carr. **Atlas Cedar** PINACEAE

Evergreen

The Atlas Cedar, introduced to Britain in 1845, differs principally from other cedars (Pl. 44, 45) in having an erect leader and ascending ends to the branches. Furthermore, it has a blue-green foliage, and may even be grey; and the cones are usually more numerous and rather smaller and less barrel-shaped. The tree's native habitat is on the mountains of Algeria and Morocco.

The trees are conical when young, later developing massive trunks and large, ascending branches. The branchlets are of two kinds: the long terminal growth shoots with needles scattered around them ('juvenile' foliage), and short spur growths with needles in rosettes. The mature needles are about an inch in length, and slightly bluish-green.

Both sexes of flowers are usually found on different branches of the same tree. The male catkins, in regimented rows, are long and erect, dull greyish-green with a purplish bloom, liberating bright yellow pollen in autumn. The females are small, greenish, erect conelets, and the resultant erect resinous barrel-shaped green cones do not reach full size until after two years, when they turn brown and ripen within a few months. They then gradually break up, releasing their winged seeds, the central spike of the cone alone remaining.

At first the bark is smooth and grey, but with age becomes brown, furrowed and scaly. The wood has a narrow whitish sapwood and a mid-brown heartwood, and is fairly hard, fragrant, naturally durable, and will work to a fine finish. It is scarce, hence little used commercially.

The variety *glauca*, a blue form in cultivation, has very pleasing blue or glaucous needles. In its most richly coloured form it is one of the most effective of all conifers, but the glaucous tint is an unstable character. It was introduced to Britain in 1845 by Lord Somers of Eastnor in Herefordshire.

44

Cedrus deodara (Roxb.) G.Don **Deodar Cedar** PINACEAE

Evergreen

The Deodar Cedar differs principally from the Atlas Cedar (Pl. 43) in having a flexible, pendulous leader; and differs from both the Atlas and the Lebanon Cedars (Pl. 45) in having longer needles, pendulous tips to the branches and larger barrel-shaped cones. Furthermore, it is a relatively taller, more graceful and erect tree than either of the other cedars. The tree is a native of the western Himalayan ranges of India, and was introduced to Britain in 1831 and 1841.

The trees are conical when young, later developing massive trunks and large often spreading branches. The branchlets are of two kinds: the long terminal gracefully drooping growth shoots with needles scattered around them ('juvenile' foliage), and short spur growths with needles in rosettes. The young needles are yellowish. The mature needles are from 1–2 inches in length, and a soft shade of green.

Both sexes of flowers are usually found on different branches of the same tree, though whole trees may be of one sex. The male catkins are long and erect, dull greyish-green with a purplish bloom, liberating bright yellow pollen in autumn. The females are small, greenish, erect conelets. The resultant erect resinous barrel-shaped green cones, up to 5 inches long, do not reach full size until after two years, when they turn brown and ripen within a few months. They then gradually break up to release their winged seeds, the central spike of the cone alone remaining.

The bark and wood are as described for Atlas Cedar (Pl. 43).

The tree has been tried experimentally in plantation form in the New Forest (1861), the Forest of Dean, and Bagley Wood in Oxfordshire – and has not fared remarkably well.

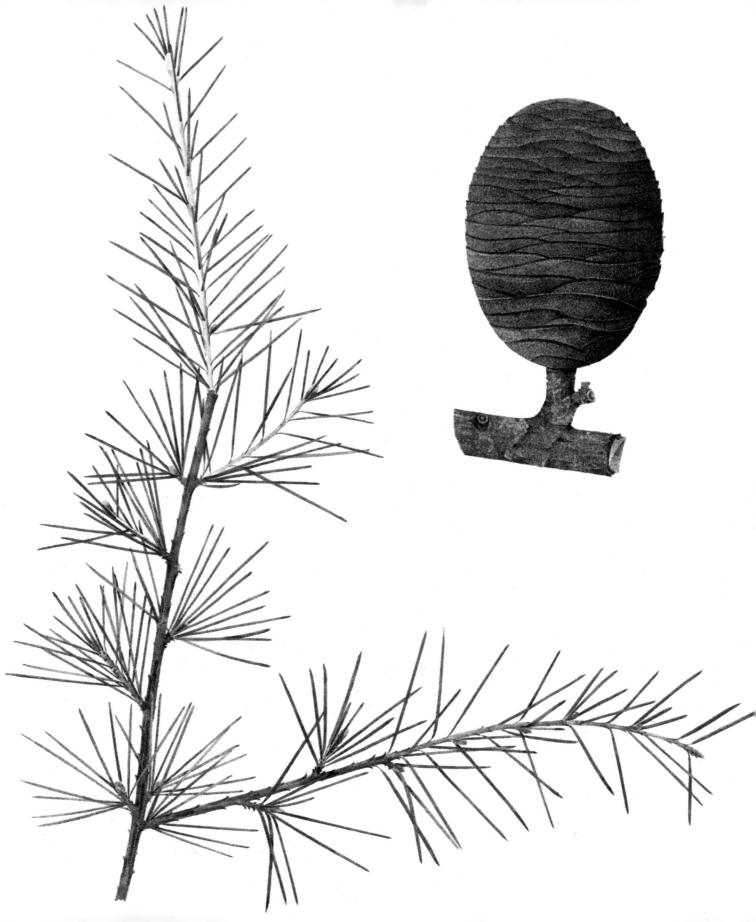

45

Cedrus libani A.Rich. **Cedar of Lebanon** PINACEAE

Evergreen

The Lebanon Cedar differs principally from the Atlas Cedar (Pl. 43) in having, later in life, a drooping or bent leader and horizontal branches forming table-like masses of needles; furthermore, it usually has grass-green needles, and the cones are rather larger and more barrel-shaped. It differs principally from the Deodar (Pl. 44) by its shorter needles, and in not having pendulous tips to the branches; furthermore it is less tall, less graceful, and not so erect, being usually a more spreading tree. The tree comes from the Lebanon mountains in Syria and the Cilician Taurus. It was introduced to Britain in 1638 but not commonly planted until 1760.

The trees are conical when young, later developing massive trunks and large, often spreading branches. The branchlets are of two kinds: the long terminal growth shoots with needles scattered around them ('juvenile' foliage), and short spur growths with needles in rosettes. The mature needles are about an inch in length, and grass-green.

Both sexes of flowers are usually found on different branches of the same tree. The male catkins are long and erect, dull greyish-green with a purplish bloom, liberating bright yellow pollen in autumn. The females are small, greenish, erect conelets. The resultant erect resinous barrel-shaped green cones do not reach full size until after two years, when they turn brown and ripen within a few months. They then gradually break up, releasing their winged seeds, the central spike of the cone alone remaining.

The bark and wood are as described for Atlas Cedar.

To be a handsome ornamental, the tree needs light and space. Only then can its wide-spreading crown on a stout trunk, wit level branches and intricate tracery of fine twigs, be fully appreciated. Old specimens particularly are among the most picturesqu evergreens, lending an aspect of dignity an beauty to parks and gardens.

46

Chamaecyparis lawsoniana Parl. **Lawson Cypress** CUPRESSACEAE

Evergreen

Lawson Cypress was introduced from the west of North America by Andrew Murray in 1854, and its name commemorates Peter Lawson, an Edinburgh nurseryman who was active in promoting botanical expeditions. It is best known as a fairly slow growing, narrow crowned tree, densely foliaged to the base, short branched with pendulous ends, one or more drooping leaders, a tendency to fork, and with thin foliage, often sold to florists for decorative purposes and the making of wreaths.

The spray-like foliage, which resembles the flattish fronds of a fern, surrounds the shoots, so that no buds are visible, and is made up of overlapping scale-like needles (more correctly, leaves) of two kinds – broad, but less so than *Thuja* – Pl. 62, on the flat surface, longer and narrow on the edge of the shoots. The shiny upper surface is usually medium- or bluish-green, but may be of other shades of green or yellow. The lower surface has a bloom of white wax. When crushed the shoots give off a strong smell resembling parsley.

The flowers of both sexes are found on the same tree. They are usually numerous and appear in March. The small, crimson and conspicuous males are tiny and club-shaped, and scatter their pollen at the end of March or in early April. The small globe-shaped females are yellowish-green, with dark tips to the scales. They soon swell to small berry-like round cones (somewhat like a pea, but with flat-topped segments), about $\frac{1}{3}$ inch in diameter, light green with a grey bloom, later ripening to blue-grey reddish-brown and opening to shed their small brown seeds in early autumn.

At first the bark is thin, greyish-brown and smooth and shiny. Later it becomes reddish-brown, irregularly fissured and peels in thin strips or flakes; within is a bright pink bark. The sapwood is yellowish white, the heartwood grey to dark brown. It is strong, light and naturally durable, and is valuable for joinery and fencing.

A popular hedgeplant and ornamental, the tree is going out of favour with foresters because of its slow growth, low volume, and tendency to fork.

There are many ornamental varieties (actually 'cultivars') based on colour or arrangement of foliage, artificially propagated, usually by taking cuttings or making grafts. For example, the variety *glauca* (a definite blue shade), *erecta* (a deep true green), and *lutea* (a bright golden yellow). There are also columnar, dwarf, fasciated and pendulous forms.

47

× *Cupressocyparis leylandii* Dallim. **Leyland Cypress** PINACEAE

Evergreen

This remarkable and interesting hybrid was first raised in 1888 by C. J. Leyland at Leighton Hall near Welshpool in Montgomeryshire, the seed parent being a Nootka Cypress, *Chamaecyparis nootkatensis* Spach., near which grew a Monterey Cypress, *Cupressus macrocarpa* Gordon. Six seedlings were seen to differ from typical Nootka seedlings and were transplanted to Haggerston Castle in Northumberland, where they grew to a considerable size without exciting any particular attention. In 1911, two seedlings of the reverse cross were raised at Leighton Hall, the female parent on this occasion being the 'macrocarpa'. It was not until 1925 that the hybrids were brought to the notice of Dallimore and Jackson, who obtained specimens for propagation and published a botanical description in the following year.

Clones from the original hybrids noted above have been propagated on an increasingly large scale, especially since the advent of mist propagation facilitated the rooting of cuttings. The commonly used clones can be distinguished by differences in habit, and in the ease of striking of their cuttings.

Leyland Cypress is a vigorous tree, densely foliaged to the base, columnar in habit, with the best characteristics of its parents. It has pleasing mid-green or blue-green sprays of foliage made up of scale-like needles, and long ascending compact branches which are red or cinnamon except for the shoots, which are green. Both sexes of flowers are found on the same tree. The round cones are intermediate between those of its parents in size ($\frac{1}{2}$–$\frac{3}{4}$ inch in diameter) and in number of scales (eight). They are greenish, and later turn to grey or chocolate brown. The seeds ripen in the second year, but propagation is almost wholly by cuttings. The timber is pale brown, of good strength, and has satisfactory working properties.

The tree is of great horticultural value, and is also a fine hedgeplant, being fast-growing and notably winter-hardy. Silviculturists too are propagating it by cuttings and planting it in tens of thousands in the hope that there may be a good future for this tree, comprising as it does the fast growth rate of Monterey Cypress with the frost hardiness and good timber characteristics of Nootka Cypress. There is one tree (at Bicton in Devon) over 100 feet tall.

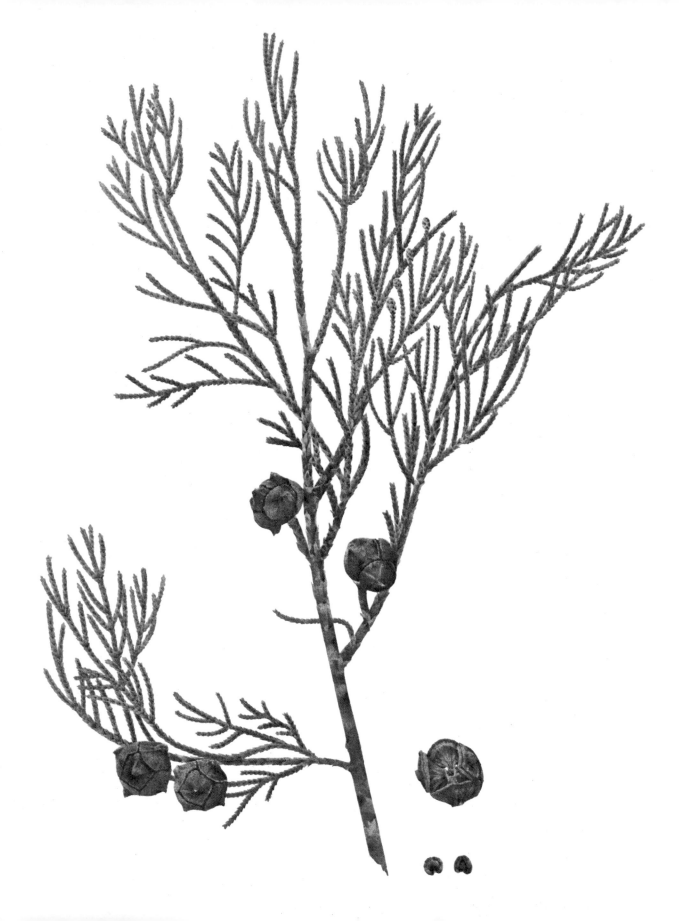

48

Larix decidua Mill. **European Larch** PINACEAE

Deciduous

European Larch, Britain's best known deciduous conifer, was introduced from Europe in 1620 but not planted on a forest scale before 1750. We appreciate it as a tree graceful in form, and of airy light foliage which reflects so well the passing of the changing seasons.

The young terminal shoots are pendulous and long, straw coloured, shallowly furrowed, and roughened in their second season by needle bases of the previous year. The brown winter buds at their tips have many scales, and are non-resinous; the buds at the sides are smaller. The short spur shoots become very dark brown, with buds that are short and rounded. The pointed needles, $1\frac{1}{4}$–$1\frac{1}{2}$ inches long, are scattered around the young shoots ('juvenile' foliage), but on the older twigs are in rosettes of twenty to thirty, all springing from a short spur shoot. They are soft and bright emerald green at first, becoming duller later, and fade to a pale straw colour before they fall in autumn.

Both sexes of flowers are found on the same tree. The flowers appear a little in advance of the needles. The small round males (found on the underside of the twigs) are clusters of golden anthers when ripe. The females are erect and usually rosy-pink – a soft conelet, which later hardens and turns cylindrical, with brown closed scales. The cones stand erect, have a tapering outline, and are 1–$1\frac{1}{2}$ inches long. They ripen by October, and their scales open, though they persist on the tree for an indefinite time.

At first the bark is thin and greyish-brown, becoming thick, brown (sometimes with a purplish sheen) and fissured longitudinally with age, when it is sometimes shed in small plates. The inner layers show a carmine-red tint. Some stems are disfigured by canker. The branches are irregular, mostly downswept from the trunk, and then upturning. The fairly narrow sapwood is yellowish, and the heartwood is reddish-brown. It is coarse in texture and resinous, but strong, hard and naturally durable, providing a multi-purpose timber, particularly used for fencing, gates, and estate repair work, also for the planking of Scottish fishing boats.

Though a well-established tree, European Larch is not widely planted now because Japanese and Hybrid Larch (Pl. 49) grow faster and are canker-free; only certain strains (some Scottish, and Sudeten) of European Larch avoid this trouble. Yet the tree is of rapid early growth, sometimes exceeding 60 feet in twenty years.

Hybrid Larch, *L. × eurolepis* Henry, an important natural cross, is referred to under Japanese Larch (Pl. 49).

49

Larix kaempferi Carr. **Japanese Larch** PINACEAE

Deciduous

This species of larch is easily distinguished from the European Larch (Pl. 48) by its blue-green foliage in summer and the reddish appearance of its bare branches in winter. It was introduced by John Gould Veitch in 1861 from Japan, where its native habitat is on the slopes of Mount Fuji and neighbouring peaks.

The young terminal growth shoots are pendulous and long, russet coloured, and by their second year are red with waxy bloom, shallowly furrowed, and roughened by needle bases of the previous year. The winter buds at their tips are reddish-brown and resinous; the buds at the sides are smaller. The pointed needles, $1-1\frac{1}{2}$ inches long, are scattered around the young shoots ('juvenile' foliage), but on the older twigs are in rosettes of twenty to thirty, all springing from a short spur shoot. They are soft and blue-green, slightly wider than those of European Larch, with two stomatal bands beneath, and they fade to a rich orange colour before they fall in autumn.

The flowers of both sexes are found on the same tree, and they are smaller than those of European Larch. They appear a little in advance of the needles. The small round brown males are set on the underside of the branches, and are pale yellow when ripe. The female conelets are erect and cream or greenish, with reflexed bracts. They later harden, and become brown, squat and broad cones, with scales which are reflexed at their edges. The cones stand erect, are rounded in outline, and are $1-1\frac{1}{2}$ inches long. They ripen by October, and their scales open though the cones persist on the tree for an indefinite time.

The bark of young trees is at first smooth and reddish, becoming thick, brown and scaly or finely fissured with age. The branches are irregular, mostly horizontal, and often the leader has a corkscrew formation, which disappears with age. The fairly narrow sapwood is yellowish, and the heartwood is reddish-brown. It is coarse in texture and resinous but strong, hard and naturally durable, providing a multi-purpose timber, particularly used for fencing, gates, and estate repair work.

Foresters appreciate this tree as a fast starter, though not, overall, a producer of very high volume. It is practically free of canker, and is useful for suppressing ground vegetation, though it will not withstand shade itself.

Hybrid Larch, *L.* × *eurolepis* Henry, is a natural cross between European Larch and Japanese Larch first raised in 1897 (accidentally) and in 1904 (deliberately) at Dunkeld in Perthshire. It first arose through the chance cross-pollination of female flowers of Japanese Larch by male flowers of the European kind. It shows remarkable 'hybrid vigour', growing faster than either of its parents, and has been planted on a considerable scale, but seed is still scarce. Its botanical characteristics are variable, but intermediate between those of the two parents.

50

Metasequoia glyptostroboides Hu et Cheng **Dawn Redwood** TAXODIACEAE

Deciduous

This fascinating and delicate looking tree owes its presence in Britain to a discovery by a Chinese botanist in 1941. Previously it had been known to science only as a fossil – hence, now, its odd name and fame as the 'fossil tree'. It grows naturally only in isolated areas in East Szechwan and West Hupeh, China, where it thrives best in shady moist localities, in ravines and on stream banks. By 1948, seedlings were being raised in Britain, and because the tree strikes fairly easily from cuttings it has since been widely planted as specimens by arboriculturists, and in a few small groves by silviculturists, as in 1953 at Leighton in Montgomeryshire, Huntley in Gloucestershire, and in 1955 at Bedgebury in Kent.

The tree has ascending branches, and persistent branchlets (reddish-brown when young) which carry green deciduous branchlets 3 inches or more in length. The small opposite winter buds are usually below the scar of the side shoot. The two-ranked needles, usually an inch or more in length, are arranged in intricate and delicate patterns. It is one of the first trees to show green in spring – a pale fresh green – later turning to bright green on the upper surface, lighter green or slightly glaucous on the under surface. Throughout summer the foliage changes through various shades of greenish-bronze, often with a pinkish tinge. In years of average autumn colours, the foliage has a moderately long spell of a yellowish pink and salmon pink before going pale brown, but in good sunny years it changes from this pink through brick-red to a rich dark rust-red. In autumn the needles are reddish-brown before they are shed along with the deciduous branchlets.

The male flower (not as yet produced in Britain) is ovoid, up to $\frac{1}{5}$ inch long; the female conelet is sub-globose or short cylindrical, about $\frac{3}{4}$ inch long, and pendulous. Some trees in Britain have grown cones from their tenth year onwards, but they have not yet produced viable seed.

The rough bark is soft and of pinkish-buff or reddish-brown shades. The older British trees are beginning to develop the picturesque ruggedness reported from China and, unfortunately for the silviculturists, to develop knotty, ridged and pocketed boles with rapid taper. The tree grows rapidly at first (up to 3–4 feet a year) and continues to do so under light shade and shelter. The tallest are already over 60 feet.

Dawn Redwood is proving a fascinating ornamental, and is particularly welcome for its spring and summer foliage, and its autumn tints. Even in winter the bare stems are enriched by the red-brown flakes of bark and pale brown, smooth stem between the raised flakes.

51

Picea abies (L.) Karsten **Norway Spruce** PINACEAE

Evergreen

Norway Spruce is one of Britain's best known conifers, being her traditional Christmas Tree. It was introduced from Europe or Scandinavia around 1500, and increasingly planted here from the seventeenth century.

The young shoots are reddish-brown to orange-red. The buds are yellow-brown, smooth, pointed, and free of resin. The needles are light to dark green, stiff, up to an inch long, four-sided, and end in a point which is not harshly sharp. They lie in a shallow plane with distinct upper and lower sides. Each needle stands on a little peg projecting from the twig and when pulled away, the peg goes with the needle, accompanied by a short strip of bark; needles that fall naturally leave their pegs behind. The new pale green needles which appear in June fringe the edges of all the branches, giving the tree its best appearance.

The flowers of both sexes are found on the same tree. The clusters of stalked male catkins are about an inch long, oval, pendulous or spreading, red at first but becoming yellow in May. The female flowers, usually higher up the tree; are small oval erect structures, stalkless and green or even crimson-coloured. After fertilisation the conelets change to green or violet-purple, and gradually turn over until in the autumn they are pendent, long cylindrical cones, becoming light reddish-brown in the process and 4–6 inches long with compact scales having a texture like tough paper. The cones, usually towards the top of the tree, fall some considerable time after most of the winged seeds have been released in mid-autumn.

The bark is reddish-brown at first, and looks smooth – though rough to the touch because of small fibrous scales or small irregularities. Later it becomes greyish-brown with a reddish sheen on the exposed side and breaks into small, thin, scales; in all but very old trees it remains thin. The tree is at first conical in shape, later developing a narrow crown, with short sometimes drooping branches. The base usually broadens and is often buttressed. The wood is tough and elastic, but has no natural durability out of doors, and its heartwood is hard to treat with preservatives. White to pale yellow in colour, without colour distinction of heartwood and sapwood, it is much used for box-making, interior joinery and carpentry, paper pulp, chipboard, pit-props, and general purposes. In the trade it is usually called 'whitewood'.

Foresters find this tree in some respects more accommodating than Sitka Spruce (Pl. 52), and it grows better than Sitka in the drier eastern parts. However, Norway Spruce in general is more sensitive to exposure, less windfirm, slower growing, and produces a smaller volume of timber. Yet it will thrive under frosty conditions in Britain where Sitka will not. In young pole-stage regimented plantations, the straw coloured leader is a prominent feature.

52

Picea sitchensis (Bong.) Carr. **Sitka Spruce** PINACEAE

Evergreen

Sitka Spruce, introduced by David Douglas in 1831, is nowadays the most extensively planted tree in British forestry. It takes its name from the small seaport of Sitka in Alaska, but is found as a native southwards from that state to north California.

The young shoots are light brown to pure white. The buds are ovoid and yellowish-brown and free of resin. The needles stand out stiffly around the shoot, and are bluish-green on the upper surface, with a prominent rib; the lower surface bears two bands of white stomata giving a blue or silvery appearance. The needles are flattened, up to $\frac{3}{4}$ inch long, and have sharp horny points. Each needle stands on a little peg projecting from the twig; when pulled away, the peg goes with the needle, accompanied by a short strip of bark. In mass the needles give the tree a faintly blue sheen.

The flowers of both sexes are found on the same tree. The stalked male catkins are about an inch long, oval, pendulous or spreading, red at first but becoming yellow. The female flowers, usually higher up the tree, are small, oval, erect structures, stalk-less and crimson-coloured; they have prominent bracts which are eventually covered by the developing scales. The cone, 2–3 inches long, and blunt-ended, has papery-textured scales with crinkled edges, and is light brown becoming whitish or pale yellow. It ripens in the first year, releasing the seeds early in autumn and then persisting on the tree for indefinite periods.

The bark is at first greyish-brown and looks smooth (though rough to the touch), later breaking into greyish-brown round scales, with somewhat raised edges (in appearance like small shallow saucers), which gradually flake away. The tree is at first conical in shape, later developing long lightly drooping branches and a rather thin crown. The base usually broadens out and is often buttressed. The wood is tough but has no natural durability out of doors; it is white to pale yellow in colour – much used for box-making, interior joinery and carpentry, shed-building, paper pulp, chipboard, pit-props, and general purposes.

Foresters appreciate Sitka Spruce as a fine forest tree for the peaty hills and moors where the rainfall is heavy. It is more resistant to exposure and possibly more wind-firm than Norway Spruce (Pl. 51), and in general faster growing, and produces a larger volume of timber. It can exceed 100 feet in thirty years, and several trees are known over 150 feet, and some exceed 20 feet in girth. Sitka, particularly in drier areas, is partially defoliated annually by the attacks of an aphis, *Elatobium abietina*, making the tree appear much thinner foliaged than Norway Spruce. High moisture requirements make it unsuitable for the drier climates and soils of the south and east of Britain.

53

Pinus contorta Douglas **Lodgepole Pine** PINACEAE

Evergreen

Lodgepole Pine, a two-needled conifer, was introduced from western North America in 1855. The name 'Lodgepole' is derived from its use by Indians as poles to support their wigwams or lodges.

The twigs are orange-brown to black, wrinkled when young. The long buds are cylindrical, resinous and blunt. The young shoots stand upright in May and June like emerald candles. The needles are stiff and in pairs, bound together at their base by a sheath consisting of membranous scales. They are of similar length, about 1–2 inches, to those of Scots Pine (Pl. 57), but are stouter, slightly twisted, and yellowish-green or mid-green. The foliage tends to be dense, with much overlapping of needles, in trees of American coastal provenances.

The flowers of both sexes are found on the same tree, and they are produced from the second year of life. The males are rather dense clusters of yellow to orange globules and the females (terminal on new shoots) are small and crimson, soon becoming reddish-purple, plum-coloured and spiky conelets. The cones on inland and northern provenances of Lodgepole Pine are often at a node two-thirds of the way up the year's shoot; but the coastal provenances are rarely bi-nodal in growth. The cone points down the shoot, is somewhat egg-shaped, about $1\frac{1}{2}$ inches in length, and the raised portion of each scale (the umbo) bears a small sharp prickle.

The bark is rather odd, being a dull brownish-black, and broken into small squarish plates divided by shallow furrows, or closely scaly. The heartwood is a pale straw colour, and there is very little contrast between heartwood and sapwood. The timber has proved a satisfactory alternative to Scots Pine for roofing, flooring, interior framing, and other joinery. Thinnings are used for paper pulp, chipboard, poles and pit-props.

In the last twenty years Lodgepole Pine has been planted on an ever-increasing scale in Scotland and North Wales because of its remarkable tolerance of poor soils, including the peaty moorlands of the wetter and cloudier western districts. Under comparable conditions it grows significantly faster than does Scots Pine, and leading shoots of 5 feet may be seen.

54

Pinus nigra maritima (Aiton) Melv. **Corsican Pine** PINACEAE

Evergreen

Corsican Pine, a two-needled fast-growing and lightly branched conifer, was introduced to Britain in 1759.

The young twigs are yellowish-brown and ridged. Later they become much roughened by the persistent needle bases. The light brown, resinous buds are up to an inch long, and are broad at their base, suddenly tapering to a sharp point. The young shoots stand upright in May and June like white-green candles. The needles are greyish-green or sage-green, 3–5 inches long, in pairs, bound together at their base by a grey sheath consisting of membranous scales. They are often twisted, and are stout, and densely arranged on the shoots.

The flowers of both sexes are found on the same tree. The male catkin-like flowers lie at the base of the young shoot, and are yellow at the time of pollination. The red females at the tips of new shoots are minute conelets which later expand to asymmetrical cones $1\frac{1}{2}$–3 inches in length, becoming shiny, hard and mid-brown; the raised portion of each scale (the umbo) bears a knob. The cones open in the spring or summer of the second year after fertilisation, and release winged seeds.

The rough, greyish to dark brown bark is fissured and flakes off. The branches are whorled, often at wide intervals. The wood is resinous and has reddish heartwood surrounded by pale brown sapwood. It is adjudged to be inferior to that of Scots Pine (Pl. 57), but can be used for similar purposes. Though not naturally durable, it takes preservative well.

Silviculturists know the tree as a wind-firm, fast grower and heavy volume producer in Britain's southern and eastern regions. It is one of the most productive species on the sandy soils in the south and south-east of England. Only strains from Corsica are recommended today.

Austrian Pine, *P. nigra* Arnold, has a more coarse, rugged, less straight appearance than Corsican Pine. Its timber is coarse, knotty and usually valueless, but as the tree is hardy and windfirm it is useful as a shelterbelt, especially along the coast.

55

Pinus radiata D.Don **Monterey Pine** PINACEAE

Evergreen

Monterey Pine, a three-needled conifer with striking bright-green luxuriant foliage, was introduced to Britain by David Douglas in 1833 and can be seen on a moderate scale in the milder parts, particularly in coastal areas where it is planted for ornament and shelter, and resists salt-laden gales. It is a native of a very limited area of wet winters and hot dry summers, the Monterey Peninsula of southern California.

The young shoots soon become green. The winter buds are light brown, up to $\frac{3}{4}$ inch long, sharply pointed and resinous. The bright emerald green needles are slender, 4–6 inches long, somewhat curved, usually in threes, but occasionally in pairs. They are bound together at their base by a sheath consisting of membranous scales.

The flowers of both sexes are found on the same tree. The male catkins are small, and yellow in late March. The female flowers may be solitary or in small clusters. The cones are asymmetrical, being flattened on that side which presses against the stem, 3–5 inches long, glossy, woody and greyish-brown. They are often in clusters of three to five, and persist on the trees for an indefinite time, usually not opening for several years.

The bark of mature trees is dark brown, thick, and deeply fissured, peeling off in broad scales. The coarse timber is inferior, and rarely used in Britain – but elsewhere for boxes, general construction and paper pulp.

This pine has no commercial future anywhere in Britain, but in South Africa, Australia, New Zealand and Spain it is cultivated on an extensive scale, making phenomenally fast growth.

56

Pinus strobus L. **Weymouth Pine** PINACEAE

Evergreen

Weymouth Pine, a five-needled conifer of the eastern half of North America, now found sparsely throughout Britain, was introduced in the eighteenth century by Lord Weymouth on his Longleat estate near Bath. It is reputed to have been first grown at Badminton, Gloucestershire, by the Duchess of Beaufort in 1705. It was the first conifer planted in the Forest of Dean (*c.* 1781). Fine needles and banana-shaped cones make this an interesting tree, but one which is frequently ruined by a rust fungus and by bark aphids.

The young shoots are slender and green, later turning greenish-brown becoming roughened by the scars left by fallen needles, but much smoother than two-needled pines. The small resin-coated buds are sharply pointed and greyish-brown. The five pendent needles are thin, 3–5 inches long, blue-green or bluish-grey, and bound together at their base by a sheath consisting of membranous scales.

The flowers of both sexes are found on the same tree. The male catkins are about $\frac{1}{2}$ inch long, and are in small clusters, yellow when ripe. The slender female flowers are about $\frac{3}{4}$ inch long, pink with purple scale margins. When young the cones are green, later becoming brown. They are pendent, slightly curved (banana-shaped), up to 6 inches long, their widely separated scales sometimes coated with white blobs of resin. Heavy crops of cones only occur at intervals of from four to seven years.

The bark on young stems is smooth and green or greenish-brown, later becoming dark grey, rough, and deeply fissured into broad, scaly ridges on the lower part of the trunk. The wood is pale brown, light, soft, and fine textured, suitable for joinery and general purposes.

The tree would undoubtedly be a fine timber-producer in southern England but for the attack of a rust fungus, *Cronartium ribicola*, which causes 'blisters' on the pine shoots and at another stage attacks black-currants and gooseberries. As it is, the tree is now rarely planted.

57

Pinus sylvestris L. **Scots Pine** PINACEAE

Evergreen Native

The hardy Scots Pine, well known by its pale red bark towards the top of the tree and its contrasting blue-green foliage, is Britain's only native conifer grown for timber production.

The buds are reddish-brown, up to $\frac{1}{2}$ inch long, narrow and blunt. The young shoots stand upright in May and June like white-green candles, smooth and shiny. Later they lengthen and turn green, becoming greyish or yellowish-brown. The stiff, blue-green needles, about 1–2 inches or more long, are in pairs, bound together at their base by a grey sheath consisting of membranous scales.

The flowers of both sexes are found on the same tree. The male flowers are small, globose catkins tightly clustered and set some way back from the tips of the twigs; at first dull red, they become golden at pollen time. The tiny female conelets are green with crimson ends to their scales, and appear in May at the very tips of newly expanded shoots. After fertilisation they grow during the next year into small green round structures. Later they become hard, woody, greyish-brown cones which are symmetrical, 'pointed', and about $1\frac{1}{2}$ inches long; the raised portion of each scale (the umbo) bears a knob. The cones mature in two years, and winged seeds fall in spring. On some trees there will be found not only one year and two year old cones, but also three year old, open and empty.

The bark at the base is fissured, forming irregular, longitudinal plates which are reddish or greyish-brown. The shining orange-red bark of the upper part of the tree is a distinct and warming feature. When young, the tree is conical and well furnished with whorls of branches; when mature, it is usually sparsely branched with a flat or domed crown.

The timber is resinous and has a distinct reddish heartwood surrounded by pale-brown sapwood. Its many uses include telegraph poles, railway sleepers, fencing, construction work, pit-props, boxes, wood wool, paper pulp, and chip-board. Though not naturally durable, it takes preservative well. In the timber trade the wood is often referred to as 'fir', 'deal' or 'redwood', usually qualified in some way.

Scots Pine is now found in its wild state only in Scotland, but has been extensively planted throughout Britain; it grows readily from self-sown seed on heaths in many southern counties. It is most successful in the warmer and drier districts towards the south and east.

As a shelterbelt tree, this pine has proved successful in the south and east and at low elevations elsewhere.

58

Pseudotsuga menziesii (Mirb.) Franco **Douglas Fir** PINACEAE

Evergreen

Douglas Fir, a magnificent, large and important tree of western North America, was discovered by Archibald Menzies, a Scottish botanist, in 1791 on the west coast of Vancouver Island. David Douglas, another Scottish botanist, sent seeds to England in 1827, and the tree now ranks as a major species in British forestry, particularly so far as speed and quantity of growth, and strength of wood are concerned. The tree is not a true fir: its cones are pendent whereas those of true firs stand erect.

The young shoots are yellowish-green (some dark pink, briefly), turning grey as they age. The brown papery buds are shiny, long and spindle-shaped, and always non-resinous. The needles are soft, disposed on a flat plane, and are deep green on top, with a groove; underneath they show two grey bands of stomata on either side of a prominent midrib. They taper towards the apex, and when pulled away from the twig they leave a smooth round scar, not a peg. The soft new pale green needles which appear in June fringe the edges of all the branches, giving the tree its best appearance.

Both sexes of flowers are found on the same tree. The male catkins are mostly pendulous and in groups; they are brownish or dull red at first, turning yellow at pollen time. The female flowers are at first erect, with soft green scales, and long pointed bracts, which are usually crimson or pink. They hang down when developing into the 2–3 inch cones which become pale-brown, with papery three-pronged bracts peering out from each scale. Winged seeds fall in mid-autumn.

The bark is at first greyish-black and smooth, with some blisters holding fragrant resin, but eventually becomes reddish-brown, thick and corky, deeply ridged and fissured, with orange-brown tints in the cracks. The sapwood is pale creamy-brown, and the heartwood pinkish-brown, darkening with age. The wood is coarse in texture, fairly hard, straight-grained, resinous, strong and heavy, providing an excellent constructional, flooring, and joinery timber, as well as one having many other uses which include fencing, pit-props, paper pulp, and telegraph poles.

Silviculturists appreciate Douglas Fir's quick growth and heavy volume, but take care not to plant it on infertile ground or where windblow may result. It is only seen at its best on deep well-drained soils in fairly sheltered situations. A specimen at Powis Castle near Welshpool in Montgomeryshire rises about 180 feet – one of the tallest trees in Britain.

The Colorado or 'Blue' Douglas Fir, *P. menziesii glauca* Franco, is a smaller and slower-growing tree with bluish foliage that smells of turpentine when crushed. This species is not satisfactory in Britain, and is planted only as a slow-growing ornamental.

59

Sequoia sempervirens (D.Don) Endl. **Redwood** TAXODIACEAE

Evergreen

Redwood provides the tallest and possibly the most majestic tree in the world – about 367 feet in California where the species lives for upwards of two thousand years. In Britain, at the comparatively young age of about one hundred and ten years, it provides our greatest volume of timber per acre – over 20,000 cubic feet (some 600 tons) in the famous 'Charles Ackers Redwood Grove' at Leighton near Welshpool in Montgomeryshire – the property of the Royal Forestry Society of England, Wales and Northern Ireland.

The native habitat of the tree is a strip, averaging some thirty-five miles wide, of the Pacific coastal regions of North America, stretching from about one hundred miles south of San Francisco up to south-west Oregon. The land ranges from sea level to some three thousand feet. *Sequoia* honours a famous half-bred Cherokee chief, Sequoyah. The tree was introduced to Britain via Russia in 1843.

The shoots are green at first, becoming brown. The buds are solitary, and surrounded by green scales which later turn brown. The secondary shoots bear flattened rigid needles spirally arranged, but with a twist at their base which brings them into two ranks. The needles produced early and late in the season are shorter than those when growth is at its height. All are slightly ribbed, and are bright green on the upper surface, and have nearly white stomatal lines underneath. Sometimes the colour of the needles is more bronze or copper than green, especially after being scorched in a cold winter. The best appearance of the tree is when the new pale green needles fringe each branch in June.

Both sexes of flowers are on the same tree, the small yellow males arising at the tips of the shoots, and the small green females well behind them. The brown elliptical cones are about $\frac{3}{4}$–1 inch long, and ripen in the first season; after opening and shedding small winged seeds the cones persist on the tree for many years.

The bark is rust or foxy-red, fibrous, soft and spongy, becoming very thick and deeply fissured with age. Underneath the bark is a hard inner layer that is bright cinnamon-red. Where side branches have fallen away, distinct cavities are left in the bark. The trunk broadens at the base and is irregularly buttressed.

The wood has a thin zone of pale yellow sapwood, and a red-brown heartwood. It is soft, strong and naturally durable – useful for interlaced fencing, garden furniture and general purposes. The tree is one of the few conifers to produce suckers. Coppice shoots arise from the stump when a tree is felled – one of the few conifers besides Yew, with this property. Blown trees left lying in the forest have been known to throw vertical shoots from the upper side of the horizontal trunk, which themselves develop into large trees, as is evident at Leighton.

Redwood has been established in plantation form in several places in southern England and Wales, where it has proved fast-growing. Silviculturists will probably plant it on a larger scale when it can be established cheaply.

Visitors to the Redwood grove at Leighton will long remember its massive pillars of warm red, with the forest floor a dull red colour. There, as also in the extensive reserved stands of the species in and near California, one cannot fail to experience a feeling of awe or indeed profound dignity and respect for this splendid tree.

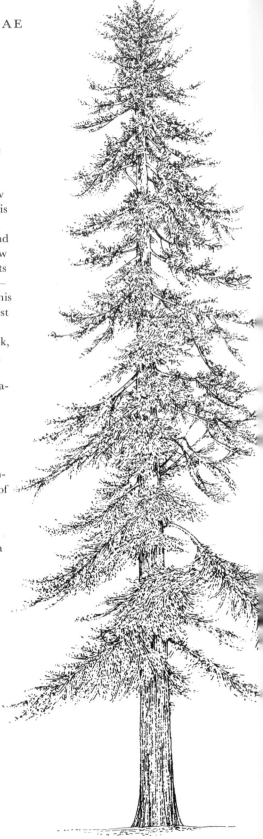

60

Sequoiadendron giganteum Bucholz **Wellingtonia, Big** or **Mammoth Tree** TAXODIACEAE

Evergreen

Wellingtonia provides the largest tree in the world – over 50,000 cubic feet (over 1,000 tons) in the Sequoia National Park in the Sierra Nevada of California: It lives for upwards of three thousand years, yet it is second in longevity to the scruffy, distorted Bristle-cone Pine, *Pinus aristata* Engelm. Many people will recall the Wellingtonia as the tree through which one could drive a car! Its native habitat is now some seventy isolated groves at between five thousand feet and eight thousand feet amid the sierras of northern California, where many of the trees stand as huge orange-coloured columns perplexing the imagination and almost defying the skill of the photographer. The tree was first introduced into Britain in 1853.

The young shoots remain covered by the needles (more correctly, leaves) for three or four years. The minute scaleless buds are hidden by the foliage. The needles are lance-shaped 'scales' which completely clothe the twigs, with a four-pointed tip, and when crushed have a minty smell.

Both sexes of flowers are on the same tree, the small club-shaped yellow males in clusters at the twig tips, and the pale green globular females, bearing spine-tipped bracts, further back. The cones are egg-shaped, made up of thick flat-surfaced green scales which do not overlap. They swell to 1–2 inches long, becoming reddish-brown, and mature in the second autumn, releasing winged seeds. Many of the empty cones persist on the tree for indefinite periods.

The fibrous bark is reddish-brown ('fox-red') to blackish-brown or grey, soft and spongy, becoming very thick and deeply fluted with age. Underneath is an inner layer that is thin and firm. Where side branches have fallen away, distinct cavities are left in the bark. The tree is conical in shape, with a tapering and broadly buttressed trunk, and with drooping branches and a narrow crown. The wood has a thin zone of pale yellow sapwood, and a reddish-brown heartwood. It is soft, strong, and naturally durable; when from time to time an individual tree is felled the wood is used for general planking, posts and garden furniture.

The towering Wellingtonia is conspicuous as an avenue and park tree, and stands out unmistakenly in the distant landscape. A few groves, as at Westonbirt in Gloucestershire, indicate that the tree might be successful in Britain in plantation form, but in general silviculturists have not planted it, perhaps chiefly on account of the high cost of plants.

The popular English name, Wellingtonia, was given in honour of the Duke of Wellington (1769–1852). Americans call it the Big or Mammoth Tree.

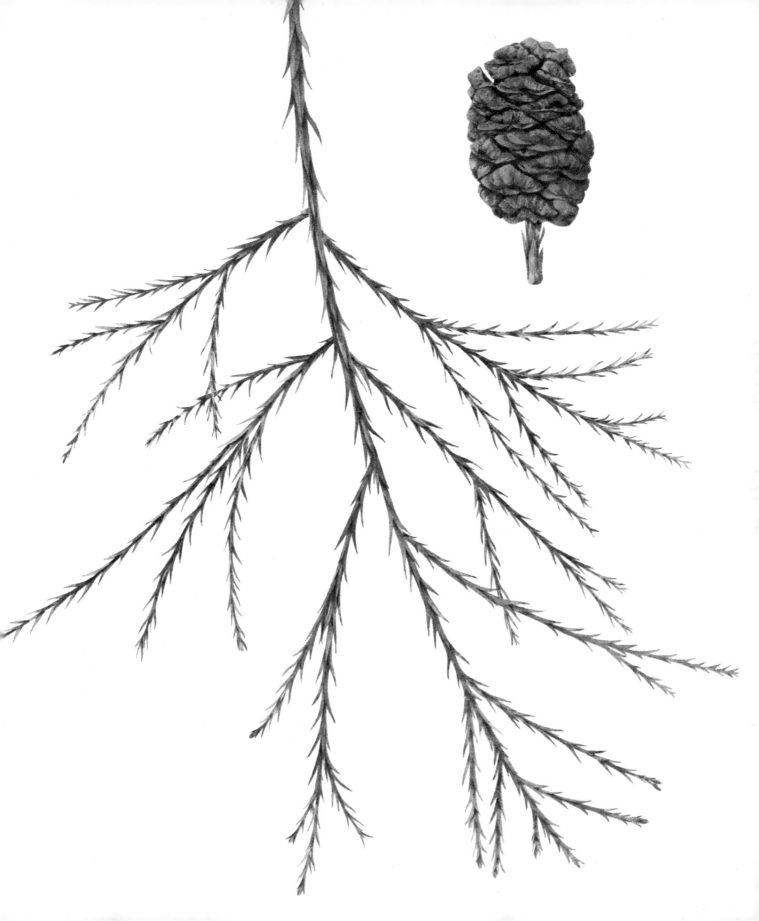

61

Taxus baccata L. **Yew** TAXACEAE

Evergreen Native

Yew ranks as one of Britain's best known conifers, having an association with bows (not arrows) and with churchyards, being a symbol of mourning, and having a wealth of legend. It ranges from old gnarled specimens in churchyards to young seedlings and isolated trees scattered throughout woodlands, and to natural groups and rows, bereft of undergrowth, appearing on chalk and limestone formations. It is usually seen as a rounded, densely branched tree, rarely of great height but often with a massive fluted trunk.

The small green buds have leafy scales that are free at the tips. The needles are arranged spirally around the green shoots, but by means of a twist they are spread into more or less two ranks. They are $\frac{3}{4}$–$1\frac{1}{2}$ inches in length, and end in a horny point. The upper surface is dark, glossy green; the lower is yellowish-green. They are waxy, though the whole tree is non-resinous.

Male and female flowers normally, but not always, grow on separate trees. The males appear as small yellow globose structures arising from the leaf axils on the undersides of branches of the previous year's growth. The females grow in similar positions but are minute and solitary consisting of greenish-yellow overlapping scales. They swell to form the spherical fruit, an olive-green hard seed surrounded by an aril, which is green at first, and in August turns to pink or scarlet, and becomes fleshy and sweet. This whole fruit lies in a dull green cup.

The bark is thin, scaly, and dark reddish or greyish-brown, becoming deeply furrowed in age, and breaking away in long flakes. The outer bark has a satiny red under-surface. The bole is often fluted. The bark, shoots, leaves, and seeds are poisonous. Coppice shoots arise from the stump when a tree is felled. The wood is very strong, tough, elastic, hard, heavy and naturally durable. The narrow sapwood is white, the heartwood deep golden or red-brown. The timber is scarce in large sizes, but may be used for posts or stakes, while craftsmen employ selected material for decorative tables, cabinets, wood sculpture and turned articles such as bowls.

From the days of the formal garden, Yew has been used for evergreen hedges. It stands unlimited clipping, and thus is the plant most used for topiary – the peculiar art of training trees into unnatural shapes. Many large, gnarled Yews in churchyards, with their tenacious hold on life, must be over seven hundred years in age.

62

Thuja plicata D.Don **Western Red Cedar** or **Arbor-vitae** CUPRESSACEAE

Evergreen

Western Red Cedar, also commonly called by its botanical name of 'thuja', and very rarely as Arbor-vitae (tree of life), was introduced to Britain by William Lobb in 1854 from western North America where it was the tree used by the Haida tribe of Red Indians for canoes and the carving of totem poles. It is a fine and popular hedgeplant, but also plays an important role in silviculture, being well known as a tall, fast growing tree with an erect leader and upward curving branches. When grown in the open it has a formal pyramidal habit, densely foliaged to the base.

The spray-like foliage, which resembles the flattish fronds of a fern, surrounds the shoots so that no buds are visible, and is made up of overlapping scale-like needles (more correctly, leaves) which are broad (more so than Lawson Cypress, Pl. 46) except those on the edges of shoots, which are narrow. The foliage is yellow-green to dark green, sometimes bronze on top, paler underneath. The shoots have a distinctive resinous, sweet fragrance when crushed.

The flowers of both sexes are found on the same tree. They are usually numerous and appear in March. The small oval dull crimson males turn yellow with pollen. The minute females have scales of pale green, tipped with black. The slender conelets develop into small upright green cones resembling a miniature Grecian urn about $\frac{1}{2}$ inch tall, comprised of leathery scales which turn brown before separating close to their base, thereby releasing the narrow-winged seeds in early autumn.

The bark is thin, cinnamon-red on young stems. Later it turns to grey or brown, and when mature develops irregular shallow fissures which divide the bark into plates which are shed, exposing the red bark underneath. The sapwood is pale yellowish, the heartwood at first bright orange-brown, weathering to an attractive silver-grey. The wood is soft, light, and naturally durable – but under British climatic conditions exposed woodwork needs preservative surface treatment about every five years. It proves valuable for joinery, greenhouse and shed construction, bungalows, ladder poles, fencing and roofing shingles.

Thuja is a very popular hedgeplant and some of its varieties make fine ornamental trees. Silviculturists like it for its quick growth and heavy volume, and for its suitability as a good underplant.

63

Tsuga heterophylla Sarg. **Western Hemlock** PINACEAE

Evergreen

Western Hemlock, also commonly called by its botanical name of 'tsuga', is a conifer of tranquillity and gracefulness, whose light lace-work of innumerable pendent branchlets, and pendent whip-like leader are making it increasingly well known in Britain. It was introduced by John Jeffrey in 1853 from the Pacific coast of North America.

The young shoots are tender, drooping at their ends, at first pale yellowish-brown, darkening to reddish-brown. The small buds are brown and ovoid. The irregular needles are $\frac{1}{3}$–$\frac{3}{4}$ inches long, have almost a round tip, and are spread in two ranks in one plane; the upper rank has the shorter needles. Their upper surface is dark green and grooved; their lower is lighter and has two bands of grey stomata on either side of a slight midrib. The new pale green needles which flush in June fringe the edges of all the branches, giving the tree its best appearance. When billowed by the wind the light, almost glaucous, underside of the foliage is exposed in mass. The foliage when crushed has an odour with a supposed resemblance to that of the hemlock plant – hence the name of the tree.

Both sexes of flowers are found on the same tree, but in different parts. The small globular crimson, then yellow male flowers lie at the bases of needles near the tips of shoots. The small females, at first green and later pink or purple, are scaly, and lie at the ends of short, erect twigs. These produce cones about $\frac{3}{4}$ inch long, that are egg-shaped and pendent. At first they are green and tinged with crimson; later they have pale brown rounded scales. Small winged seeds are released early in autumn. Empty cones persist on the tree for many months.

The bark is at first russet-brown and smooth except for fine scales. Later it becomes darker and deeply furrowed into scaly ridges. The trunk thickens abruptly at the base, and is somewhat fluted. The wood is pale yellow-brown, with a somewhat darker heartwood, fairly strong and of a fine texture. It is used for joinery, box-making, paper pulp and many general purposes.

Foresters value 'tsuga' as a fast producer of a heavy volume of timber and as an important underplant – indeed it prefers dappled shade and is difficult to establish on bare ground.

The Eastern Hemlock, *T. canadensis* (L.) Carr., is slow-growing and useless as a timber-tree in Britain, but not infrequently planted for ornament.